ב"ה

RAV DOVBER PINSON

WRAPPED

IN

MAJESTY

TEFILLIN

: Exploring the Mystery

IYYUN PUBLISHING

Published by IYYUN Publishing
232 Bergen Street
Brooklyn, NY 11217

http:/www.IYYUN.com

Iyyun Publishing books may be purchased for educational, business or sales promotional use. For information please contact: contact@IYYUN.com

cover and book design: Rochie Pinson
cover photography: Rebecca Weiss. Rebecca Weiss Photography

pb ISBN 978-0-9852011-8-0

Pinson, DovBer 1971-
Tefillin: Wrapped in Majesty / DovBer Pinson
1. Judaism 2. Spirituality 3. Ritual and Practices

This book on *Tefillin* was written in honor of the
Bar Mitzvah of our dear eldest son, young in years yet
wise in life, Yisrael Mendel, *Sheyichye.*

CONTENTS

OPENING

OPENING

A boy becomes a *Bar Mitzvah* on his thirteenth birthday. Thirteen is the numerical value of the word *Ahavah*, love, and this book is an offering of love. Thirteen is also the value of the word *Echad*, one, implying unification.

A sign of a mature person is that he is internally unified and aligned; his thoughts and feelings are consistent with his words and actions. As a child becomes a *Bar Mitzvah*, he becomes a mature individual, a more focused and unified person.

This book will explore *tefillin* from all four perspectives or lenses of the Torah, known by their acronym, *PaRDeS*, meaning orchard. They are:

1) *Peshat* — literal observation,
2) *Remez* — allegorical interpretation,
3) *Derush* — homiletic meaning, and
4) *Sod* — secret or Kabbalistic explication.

The Torah is called *Toras Echad*, a unified Torah, given and revealed to us by *Hashem Echad*, the One Infinite Source. To focus on only one dimension of *PaRDeS*, or one form of interpretation to the exclusion of the others, creates separation and disunity. Similarly, to omit any one level or mode of interpretation from the whole system would render one's understanding incomplete. For example, to view the Peshat, Remez, and Derush without the Sod, the acronym would then become *PiRuD* or separation. Each part of the Torah is a part of the whole, and to fully grasp any part, we must aspire to grasp the unified whole.

Correspondingly, the complex structure of one's self is also comprised of various dimensions:

1) the *nefesh* or physical dimension,
2) the *ruach* or emotional aspect,
3) the *neshamah* or mental sphere, and
4) the *chayah* or spiritual reality of self.

Ultimately, what we are is the unified totality of all of our multiple facets. Acknowledging only one dimension of our self at the expense of the others is, in fact, self-neglect.

The PaRDeS acronym can then be understood to reflect multiple layers of the One Reality; at once mirroring the four levels of Torah, the four levels of our Consciousness, and the four worlds of Creation, which in turn reflect the four letters of the Name of the Hashem, the Yud-Hei and Vav-Hei.

The *peshat*, or literal meaning of Torah, mirrors our *nefesh* and physical body. The *remez*, or allegorical hints and suggestions, corresponds to *ru'ach*, the emotional self. The *derush*, or homiletic interpretation, reflects the mental level of our *neshamah*, as it is a weaving together of intellectual patterns, underlying themes, and etymologies. The *sod*, or secret and mystical dimension of Torah, is a reflection of the deeper mystery hidden within each one of us, the intuitive, spiritual reality called *chayah*.

These four ways of understanding Torah and self are also reflected in the compartments of the *Tefillin Shel Rosh*, the head tefillin, which are four, yet compressed to appear as one, revealing their essential unity.

This leads us to the fifth dimension of Torah, which contains and unifies all the others in a seamless whole. It can be called the *sod she-b'sod*, the secret within the secret. This is where the *peshat* is one with the *remez (P'si'osav Shel Avraham Avinu, Os 62)*, and where the *peshat* is in total alignment with the *sod (Even Sheleima, 8:21)*. This essential level corresponds to the *yechidah* or unified reality, to *Adam Kadmon* or Primordial Man, and also the crown on top of the letter Yud of Hashem's four-letter name. When we perceive the four dimensions of PaRDeS as one unified whole, each dimension blends into every other and the unified essence of One, the *yechidah*, is revealed.

Like the cubical tefillin, *PaRDeS* represents four sides of one reality. The *peshat* flows into the *sod*, and the *sod* into the *peshat*, revealing their integral unity. In the following chapters, we will explore the reality of *tefillin* through these four lenses of interpretation, and in so doing, we may gain a glimpse of true unity.

THE BASICS OF TEFILLIN
INCLUDING BASIC KAVANAH

THE BASICS OF TEFILLIN
INCLUDING BASIC KAVANAH

*"You shall love Hashem, your G-d, with all your heart, with all your soul, and with all your might. And these words which I command you today shall be upon your heart... You shall bind them as an **Os** – a sign – upon your hand, and they shall be for **Totefos** – a reminder – between your eyes"*
(Devarim, 6:8).

Although, as mentioned, there are many dimensions to the words of the Torah, and it would be entirely plausible that the above injunction could be interpreted metaphorically *(Rashbam,* Shemos, 13:9*)*, these words have been, and are indeed meant to be, taken literally.

And so, just as we are commanded, we take hand-written inscriptions of chapters of the Torah and ritually place them on our physical body; one on the head as a reminder between the eyes and the other as a sign on the arm situated against the heart.

These are the powerful spiritual tools we call Tefillin. The actual word Tefillin itself is not found in the Torah. Instead the Torah refers to them as *Totefos* and *Os*. And yet, for thousands of years they have been called Tefillin.

But what exactly are Tefillin? On the most basic level, Tefillin consist of two cube-shaped, black leather boxes with black leather straps hanging down, which attach the boxes to the body of the wearer. The *Tefillin Shel Rosh* or Tefillin of the head, attaches snugly to the head, and the *Tefillin Shel Yad* or Tefillin of the hand, wraps tightly around the arm.

Each of these boxes contain the four paragraphs of the Torah that mention the command to wrap tefillin: *Devarim* 6:49 and 11:13-21, and *Shemos* 13:1-10 and 13:11-16. These paragraphs are carefully hand-written on small parchments by a professional *Sofer* or scribe, and inserted into the boxes.

There is, however, a basic difference between the two boxes. When the Torah describes the hand tefillin it uses a singular term, *Os*. But for the head tefillin, it uses a plural word, *Totefos*. Thus, each of the four Torah paragraphs in the head tefilin is written on its own individual scroll and inserted into one of the four small compartments.

By contrast, in the hand tefillin, all four chapters are inscribed on a single scroll and placed in one single compartment.

Having four compartments in the head tefillin is the received tradition from Sinai, but even so, numerous sages of the Talmud have given over their interpretive explanations for this specific construction.

Rabbi Yishmael teaches that the Torah hints at this arrangement by referring to the head tefillin in the plural language mentioned above, *Totefos*, even going so far as to include an extra letter Vav in its spelling to indicate its doubled nature. But Rabbi Akiva said: We do not need [this exegesis], for *Tot* in Coptic means two, and *Phos* (Fos) in African (Phrygian) means two, equaling four. So included in the very word Totefos is a combinahtion of two foreign words meaning two and two *(Menachos, 34b, Sanhedrin 4b)*.

These four compartments are then carefully pressed together to maintain the singular cube-like shape of the tefillin.

FOUR COMPARTMENTS OF THE HEAD TEFILLIN

The Meiri writes that the head is the seat of four of the senses: seeing, hearing, smelling, and tasting. Accordingly, the head tefillin has four compartments, containing four scrolls. As the hand is connected to the remaining fifth sense, touch, the hand Tefillin has a single compartment, with but one scroll *(Meishiv Nefesh, 2:2)*.

From another perspective, the Maharal writes that there are various compartments in the head tefillin, the tefillin of the intellect, and there is one compartment in the hand tefillin, the tefillin of action *(Gevuras Hashem)*. This relates to the fact that we discern, separate, evaluate, and differentiate with our intellect, whereas action is more one-dimensional, especially if it is empty of thought or emotion (i.e. awareness).

The four compartments and the Torah portions inside them can be linked to the four parts of the brain: the right and left hemispheres, the frontal lobe, and the cerebellum in back.

In general, the left hemisphere controls the function and movement of the right side of the body, while the right hemisphere controls the left side of the body. Furthermore, the left hemisphere is associated with speech. Thus, damage to it can compromise a person's ability to speak. The left hemisphere also specializes in detailed analysis, processing external data in a sequential manner.

The right hemisphere represents the more creative aspect of thinking. It functions by grasping and processing abstract patterns holistically. The right hemisphere also controls the processing of spatial and visual ideas, such as the qualities of shapes and pictures. People who have lost the function of the right side of their brain tend to lack comprehension of conventional sayings, such as, 'You are what you eat'. Such a phrase is meaningless if only digested word-by-word, rather than as a whole contextual statement.

Chochmah or non-verbal wisdom and intuition, is embodied in the right hemisphere. *Binah*, the capacity to reason and break down ideas into details and language, is embodied in the left hemisphere. *Da'as*, knowing or consciousness itself, is seated primarily in the frontal lobes of the brain, connecting and coordinating the right and left hemispheres. Da'as is the 'executive mind', in charge of making judgments and choices, planning and implementing decisions.

Some sources speak of Da'as as connected to the back of the brain *(Torahs Chayim,* Shemos, 395b*)*. This would suggest a headquarters in the cerebellum, a region that assists in coordinating muscle coordination, movement, and balance. Indeed, the energy of Da'as creates balance. In the Tree of Life diagram, Da'as inhabits the middle column and connotes balanced intellectual intelligence.

In Chapter Three, we will explore the *Koach Ha-m'damah*, the power of imagination. Here, suffice it to say that the *koach ha-m'damah* has no single location in the brain, but rather it involves any region of the brain that corresponds with what is being imagined. For example if one imagines a math problem, the prefrontal cortex is activated. If one imagines playing a physical sport, the motor cortex is involved. These specific areas are joined by activity in the more primitive, 'reptilian' regions of the brain, like the hippocampus. The neo-cortex and thalamus are also areas involved in imagination. In other words, the power of imagination involves all three energies of Chochmah, Binah and Da'as.

There are also four general brain wave types — Beta, Alpha, Theta, and Delta — relating again to the four compartments of the head tefillin. When we are alert and attentive to any external stimuli, or when we exert mental effort, we are in a Beta brain wave state. The Alpha state is when we are awake but relaxed. Daydreaming, fantasy, imagination, inspirational thinking, is a Theta state. Pure unconsciousness and deep, dreamless sleep are expressions of a Delta wave state. Thus we could say that the compartments of the head tefillin link with and influence all of our potential states of consciousness, all of the regions of our brain, and all of our mental and intellectual capacities.

COLOR & DESIGN

Many of the basic laws of the design of the tefillin are defined as *Halacha l'Moshe m'-Sinai*, traditions given by Moshe at Sinai. Among the laws in this transmitted tradition are the ten principles of writing the tefillin scrolls and how they should appear *(Rambam,* Hilchos Tefillin, 1:3*).* There are also rules of design such as that the tefillin must be square and the straps must be painted black *(Menachos,* 35a*)*, there must be protruding letter Shins on the head tefillin *(35b, Tosefos)*, and the knots of the straps must form the shape of a letter Dalet and a letter Yud *(Rashi ad loc.)*.

This halachic tradition also includes deeper layers of meaning encoded into the physical form of the tefillin. These symbols and explanations from various perspectives will be explored later on in this text. For now, let us mention as an example, the rich symbolism of the two protruding letter Shins on the head tefillin.

On a *peshat,* or literal, level, the shape of the letter Shin is pressed into the leather of the head tefillin as a reminder of the number of days we wear tefillin throughout the year. The numerical value of the letter Shin is 300, and there are at least 300 days in the solar cycle of the year that we wear tefillin. This is true even in the Diaspora, where there are more days of Yom Tov than in Israel, and it is true even for those who put on tefillin during Chol ha-Moed, the intermediary days during the Holidays, during which most people do not wear tefillin. When we subtract the 52 Shabbosim of the year, and the 13 days of Holidays — 2 days of Rosh Hashanah, 1 day of Yom Kippur, 4 days of Sukkos, 4 days of Pesach, and 2 days of Shavuos — there remain at least 300 days *(Rabbeinu Bachya,* Devarim, 28:10*).*

On one side of the head tefillin the Shin has three prongs, according to the usual form of the letter, while the Shin on the other side of the cube has four prongs. The Shin with three prongs is how the letter is written in the Torah scroll. The Shin with four prongs, which correspond to the four protruding sides that are created within the 'white fire', or negative space, when the letter is carved into a substance, alludes to the letter Shin as it was carved into the Luchos, the sapphire tablets from Mount Sinai *(Taz, Orach Chaim, 32:35)*.

One experiential function of the two Shins on the tefillin is that we should gaze at these letters before we don the head tefillin. The Zohar teaches that we should look at the Shins of the Tefillin before we put them on *(Zohar III, 274a)*. The mere act of looking at the Shins brings down a special light, or illumination, that will assist us in remaining focused on the tefillin while wearing them *(Ben Yehoyadah, Shabbos, 118b)*.

The three and four prongs allude to how long we should wear tefillin during *tefilah,* or prayer. The Ramah writes that we should keep our tefillin on until after we have recited the three *Kedushas* and the four *Kaddeishim (Orach Chaim, 25:13. Darchei Moshe, 25:3)*.

Tefillin are also generally connected to the rhythm of cosmic time. The Zohar writes that the seven cumulative prongs of the Shins correspond to the seven thousand year cycle of this stage of creation *(Zohar III, 228b)*.

The seven prongs also correspond to the seven branches of the Menorah, a source of light and illumination *(Zohar III, 274a)*.

In a more inward and personal analogy, the Chassidic teachers write that the seven prongs of the Shins correspond to the seven orifices of the face: two ears, two eyes, two nostrils, and one mouth. These openings are understood as the physical manifestations of the seven lights, or branches, of the Menorah, with the body as the trunk and base of the Menorah itself.

In the course of this text we will delve deeper into the symbolism of the Shins and the various reasons why the tefillin needs one Shin with three prongs and one with four prongs. The reasons mentioned above bring up many deeper questions. What do all of these ideas have to do with tefillin? What do they reveal about the life-changing and mind-illuminating energy of tefillin?

BASIC KAVANAH

For now, let us begin with the basic and fundamental *Kavanah,* or intention, when putting on the tefillin. Tefillin, unlike most *Mitzvos* of the Torah, need proper intention. There are some opinions that suggest that Mitzvos do not need intention, and one is able to fulfill their obligation even without Kavanah. This is not so with tefillin. Everyone agrees that in the case of tefillin — there is no Mitzvah without intention. We need intention when putting on tefillin (*Bach, Aruch Hashulchan*, Siman 25:8).

So what is the basic intention?

The Alter Rebbe writes in his Siddur that when putting on the tefillin we should have in mind that the Holy One commanded us each to write these four portions of Torah and place them within the boxes of the tefillin. These four portions of Torah contain verses that describe the unity of Hashem, as well as the going out from Egypt, so that we remember the miracles and wonders Hashem did for us, which display Hashem's ultimate unity and mastery of all creation, from the highest heights to the deepest depths.

The Mitzvah is to place the tefillin on the arm facing in towards the heart, and on the head above the brain so that we remember to submit the soul, which is one with the mind, as well as the desires and thoughts of our heart, and the strength of our bodies to Hashem. By putting on the tefillin we will be mindful of the presence and blessings of the Creator and thus curb our ego-based appetites and pleasures.

We place the hand tefilin upon the left arm so that it rests near the heart, and the head tefillin is placed above the forehead, between the eyes so it rests against the skull — near the brain. Thus mind, heart, and actions are all aligned, unifed, and directed towards Heaven.

We are all given the gift of an expansive mind, a passionate heart, and a strong body and we can use our innate talents for mere survival, meeting only our physical needs, as the rest of the natrual world, or we can elevate ourselves, utilizing and dedicating our minds, hearts, and bodies to strive for deeper meaning in moral and spiritual growth and development. Tefillin literally impress upon us and gently demand that we utilize our minds, hearts, and actions for this higher and deeper purpose.

CHAPTER I: PESHAT
THE VISCERAL EFFECT OF TEFILLIN

CHAPTER I: PESHAT
THE VISCERAL EFFECT OF TEFILLIN

"You shall love Hashem, your G-d, with all your heart, with all your soul, and with all your might. And these words which I command you today shall be upon your heart...You shall bind them as an Os – a sign – upon your hand, and they shall be for Totefos – a reminder – between your eyes."

(Devarim, 6:8)

These signs, these reminders worn on the hand and head are called tefillin. One important derivation of the term tefillin is the Hebrew word *Pelili*, meaning an indication, for the tefillin are worn as "a sign that the Divine presence rests upon us when we wear them" *(Rosh*, Hilchos Tefillin. *Tur*, O'C, 25).

Additionally, the word is connected with the root word *Pelah*, a wonder, indicating something distingushed, separate, or unusual. As the act of putting on the tefillin distinguses us a little beyond the usual and connects us with the Trancendent One.

The word tefillin has been often translated as phylacteries, and this is very misleading, for phylacteries suggest some form of amulet or superstitious protection (Note: *Shabbos,* 57a, regarding the word *Totefos).* The simple purpose of tefillin is that they are a reminder. The tefillin serve to remind, connect, bind and dedicate our mind, heart, and body to the Creator. The Hebrew word tefillin is also related to the root word *Tofel,* to connect, join, or attach. Through the act of putting on tefillin we connect to and bind ourselves with the Creator of the universe.

Tefillin is an outward *Os,* a sign, of this connection, our joining with and attachment to Hashem. It is an external symbol of our internal intention to actualize our relationship and connection to G-d.

Besides being an external sign, it is also an external reminder, a symbol that reminds us of the everlasting and permenant connection we have with Hashem whether we wrap tefillin or not. In this way, tefillin are both a sign that signifies our acknowledgment of the unbreakable bond between us and Hashem, as well as a physical reminder of that which is always there, and thus in danger of being taken for granted, the ever-omni-presence of the Infinite One.

To truly imprint the words, wisdom, and principles of the Torah within our hearts, it is not sufficient to just think about or intellectualize its essential teachings, nor is the mere repetition of its words an adequate method of deep in-

ternalization. But through the experience of actually performing an action day in and day out, coupled of course with
deep contemplation and complex conversation, the true
teachings of the Torah become available to be accessed and
animated in a multi-dimensional and holistic fashion. The
non-verbal, experiential power of the action, along with the
repetition, ensures that the words of the Torah truly become
indelibly imprinted upon our souls for us to know in order
to live by them, as well as to teach our children and others.
As the passage says, *"You shall love Hashem, your G-d, with
all your heart…and you shall teach [these teachings] to your children… and You shall bind them as an Os upon your hand"* —
the loving, the teaching, and the binding are all inter-con-
nected.

THE KNOT OF THE TEFILLIN

Besides the actual putting on of the tefillin, the act of making a knot is symbolic of binding and strenthening a connection, ensuring that two partners do not part ways. It is
taught that people have been known to knot a string to help
them remember an event, sight, or sound, so that the past is
not forgotten in the present or future (See *Tur*, Orach Chaim,
24).

In this way the person is connecting the individual mo-
ments of their experience by tying the past to the present in
order to bring it into the future. Indeed, an outward action
effects an inward movement. In the words of the Chinuch,

"After action, the heart follows". Doing a physical activity creates the conditions within one's inner-space for the initiation of a new or desired reality — this is the power of a symbolically charged spiritual practice.

Altough we do not actually tie the knots of the tefillin anew each day, there is an opinion that we should *(Tosefos, Menachos*, 35b). In practice, we do not actually do this, but the tightening of the knot as we put the tefillin on each time is as if we are making the knot anew. In this way, everytime we bind the tefillin as an Os upon our hands we are making a knot to remind us of the relationshiop we have with Hashem. The actual act creates the reminder and we re-memeber that we are always connected.

In addition, the knot of the head tefillin is placed right beneath the skull, on top of what is called the cerebellum or 'little brain'. The Ramban writes that we place the knot of the tefillin above 'the end of the brain', that which protects memory *(Ramban,* Shemos, 13:16). Today, science knows that conscious episodic memory retrieval is connected with the cerebellum. This is the 'little brain' that is connected with memory (R. Meir Papirosh, *Torah Ohr,* Bo. *Ha'Emek Davar.* Shemos, 32:9).

Some time ago, a scientific periodical that explored the various compartments of the brain was shown to the Mitteler Rebbe, Rabbi DovBer of Chabad. In the journal it was written that if one desires to recall something to memory, one tilts the head backwards, facing up. Upon reading this, the Rebbe walked over to his bookshelves, removed a Sefer, book, and indicated that this same idea was intimated many years prior, according to Kabbalah, in this teaching that the 'little brain' — the 'end of the brain' at the base of the skull — is connected with memory (See also, *Shevilei Emunah*, Nosiv 4, 151). The placement of this knot, at the base of the skull, can thus be understood as a knot that serves to secure memory.

WHOLE BODY PRAYER

The word tefillin resembles the word *Tefilah*, prayer, for the two share the same root, which defines their common purpose in connecting us with Hashem. And although tefillin may be donned the entire day, provding one is able to remain physically and mentally pure and mindful of them throughout that period of time, it has been the custom for many hundreds of years to wear tefillin primarily during Tefilah, the time of morning prayer. "The optimum Mitzvah is to wear the tefillin the entire day, yet, during Tefilah is the most important" *(Rambam,* Tefillin, 4:5). Indeed, today most people wear tefillin only during Tefilah and the reading of the Shema *(Shulchan Aruch,* O'C, 25:4. *Berachos,* 14b).

There is the level of purely verbal prayer where our minds, heart, and lips pray. And then there is the whole-body level of tefilah where we are wrapped in tefillin. In this state of total body connection and engagement we may even visualize, says Reb Pinchas of Koritz, that our prayers are rising upwards — straight to the Heavens — through the head tefillin, the funnel and portal of our prayers *(Imrei Pinchas)*.

In this state, wrapped in tefillin, our whole body is praying. We are literally tied to Hashem — head, heart, and hand — with our physical body and our soul's purpose all knotted up and intertwined. As we are wearing the Os or sign, in a way we become one with that sign, and ultimately, in a way we become, as if, the sign itself, a living breathing signifier of the Divine's presence in the world.

TEFILLIN AS MERKAVAH

To further illustrate this idea of tefillin empowering us to reveal Hashem's presence in the world we can look to the the twelve tribes of Israel, descended from the twelve sons of Yaakov. After the Exodus from Egypt, when the Israelites encamped in the desert with a sense of unity and joined purpose, they reflected the *Merkvah*, the holy chariot, as seen by Yechezkel in his prophetic vision. The tribes joined in such a harmonious configuration also revealed Hashem's glory. In the vision of Yechezkel he sees the Heavenly Throne, as it were, and it is carried by four angelic beings with four different faces — a bull, a lion, the face of a man, and an eagle.

The twelve tribes were subdivided into four groups, three tribes in each group, arranged in the four directions. In the center of this structure was the *Mishkan*, the portable dwelling place of the revealed presence of the *Shechinah*. The tribes on the four sides of the Mishkan embodied the qualities of the Merkvah, carrying, as it were, the Shechinah within.

Each grouping of three tribes had a flag. To the west, the flag depicted the image of an ox. To the east, the flag depicted the image of a lion. To the south, the flag depicted *Dudaim* plants, mandrakes, whose roots bear an uncanny resemblance to the image of a human. And to the north, was the image of an eagle.

When we wear tefillin, we are also becoming an aspect of the Merkvah, as we are revealing Hashem's presence in the world. The "Name of Hashem is called upon us" when we wear the head tefillin *(Berachos, 6a)*. We bear and wear the very structures, the *batim*, that house the name and presence of Hashem.

And so too, the tefillin themselves, in their structure and makeup, resemble the Merkvah and the encampment of the tribes. There are four sides to the boxes of the tefillin, and each side contains three stitches. These correspond to the four camps with three tribes in each camp. So each box of tefillin wrapped around our body is thus an Os, a sign, of our collective mission, to reconnect creation back to the Creator in a bond of loving unity.

HARNESSING THE ANIMAL WITHIN

This tying of an Os upon our bodies by using, the *Ohr*, skin, of a Kosher animal is a very visceral and earthy reminder that our entire self, including our body and all its natural desires — the animal within us — is bound to Hashem, to a life of higher purpose and deeper meaning.

Instead of being tied, as we normally are, to our every whim, instinct, or subconscious desire, we untie these knots by binding ourselves to our higher purpose, principles, and values through the act of wrapping tefillin. In deed, such an unconscious state of mind, which can enslave us if we are not self-aware, is referred to as our inner *Mitzrayim* or Egypt, our place of *Metzar,* or constriction and pettiness. This is the inner reason why we recall the going out from Egypt as we put on our tefillin.

On a simple level, when we wrap ourselves in the straps of the tefillin of the hand it lessens our arms ability to move about freely. This binding suggests that our arms are tied, directed, focused, and guided by the tefillin and the messages they contain — namely the *Shema*, the declaration of Hashem's unity, written in the box of the tefillin. We bind our hands, the vehicle of our externalized strength and physical power, demonstrating that we are bending our physical prowess to a higher power, the Creator, in order to manifest our soul's mission and life's purpose. Only in this way do we gain true power.

Our arms can extend in any which direction, with or without any mindfulness or intention. We have free choice to use are arms to construct, to build, to help, to give charity. And we also have the ability to use our arms to destroy, break, hurt, steal, or take what is not one hundred percent rightfully ours. Each morning we put on the tefillin and wrap the straps around our arms, thereby demonstrating our commitment to behavior consistent with our deepest principles.

People tend to use the words power and force interchangeably when in fact they refer to two very different states. Power is the consequence of a deeper alignment with the Supreme Power of the universe. Conversely, the use of force or coercion is a symptom of powerlessness and neediness. Those who demand to be served, obeyed or esteemed usually have low self-esteem. The powerless individual forever feels the need to control, perpetually seeking to accumulate as much wealth or influence as possible, always afraid of loss and losing.

Truly powerful people emulate the Supreme Power, the Creator, by not only tolerating, but actually supporting and coordinating the abundant diversity of Creation. Real power is not over others, but for others.

HEAD, HEART & HANDS

By wrapping the straps of the tefillin around our upper arm, we are placing the actual box of the tefillin, which faces inwards, in close proximity to our heart, which is symbolically the seat of our emotions. This positioning demonstrates that not only are our physical actions being harnessed towards a higher purpose by tying our force to power as it were, but even our subtle emotions are being brought under our conscious direction. Therefore, with the wrapping of the *tefillin shel yad* we bind our hands to our hearts to ensure that our actions and emotions are consistent with the values and principles we profess.

Additionally, by wrapping the head tefillin around our skull — the proverbial throne of our consciousness —we are binding our minds up in this multi-dimensional divine knot of awareness and intention. Perhaps we do not (yet) have full control over what thoughts arise — much like many do not have control over their emotions — but we all have a choice of whether or not to indulge in any given thought; to keep on thinking that thought once it has emerged, whatever the thought is, or to redirect our awareness and replace it with another thought. It is within our power to actively replace negative or destructive thoughts or images with positive and life affirming thoughts and ideals. For instance one may choose to think about Hashem's indivisible and unique Unity or *Yichud* instead of fixating on apparent *Pirud,* or separation, strife, and ego.

The *tefillin shel rosh* are silently speaking to us as we wear them: "You do have control. You do have freewill. You do have choice. Choose Life."

Imagine, for instance, when you are very thirsty. The only thought that you can think of is about the drink. Any other thought that enters your mind is naturally discarded. So we do have control. If one can enter into a state of *Deveikus*, conscious cleaving to Hashem, with a visceral intensity through prayer, song, or study one may achieve the rectified state of a naturally reset awareness, focused on the presence of divine themes, even in the apparently mundane. So instead of being a slave to nature's call, as it were, one would be able to evolve into an attentive servant to the call of the spirit. Wearing tefillin help us move closer to achieving that state of consciousness.

Our hands/actions, hearts/emotions, and mind/intellect can all be harnessed, focused, and directed to imagine, feel, and physically express the deepest truth of who we are and why we are put on this earth.

PHYSICAL KNOWING

When the Torah describes the putting on tefillin it says;

"And it [the tefillin] shall be for a sign to you on your arm, and a memorial between your eyes, so that the Torah of Hashem may be in your mouth..." (Shemos, 13:9)

According to this passage, it would seem that the tying of the tefillin to our hand and head ensures that the Torah is in our mouth. But what does this mean?

From a legal, *halachic*, standpoint, what is alluded to in the words, "in your mouth", is the fact that the tefillin can only be produced from the skin of a kosher animal, i.e. from that which is "permitted to your mouth" *(Shabbos, 28b)*.

In addition to this interpretation about the appropriate materials for constructing the tefillin, there is something more that is being conveyed in the Torah's words, "in your mouth". The verse is implying that by putting on tefillin we are ensuring that the Torah is on 'the tip of our tongues'. We are confirming that the Torah we learn is permanent, sharp, clear, and always readily available to recalled, communicated, or put into practice (See *Kidushin, 30a*).

The act of putting on tefillin initiates the integration of information, making sure that what we know in our minds is also felt in our hearts and expressed through our actions. There is thus a total integration, where information becomes transformational. This transformation is understood as the cognitive shift from the consciousness of the 'Tree of Knowledge' to the holistic awareness of the 'Tree of Life'. This is the state of transparent knowing where ideas of the mind are immediately manifest in action.

The transformation is absolute, so that even our bodies, i.e. our natural instincts, are aligned with our deeper sense of spiritual understanding and purpose.

Many times a passing thought enters our mind and we know it is a true thought, a Torah thought, for it resonates deeply within us, and yet, our minds are so pre-occupied with other apparently pressing issues — a mortgage, a late payment, relationships, social life — that the thought or insight just comes and goes. We need to learn how to focus our attention in order to hold onto and harness positive, life affirming thoughts, and learn to release and let go of negative or destructive thoughts.

Sometimes our minds understand what we should or should not do, what is good for us and what is not — whether physically, emotionally, mentality or spiritually — and yet, our hearts and our emotions are in conflict with what we understand to be true. For example: You know and understand that flaring up in anger when your ego is hurt is neither a positive nor productive emotional expression, and yet, sometimes your reactive emotions get the better part of you.

Than there are times when our minds and hearts are unified — we understand what is good and we have trained our emotional responses to be non-reactionary — and yet, when caught off guard our instincts are inconsistent with our mindset and emotional state. So, even if most of the time you know how to handle the situation when you sense that your anger is rising up and you are being provoked, sometimes, you are completely not prepared and you're unconscious, knee jerk response is anger.

The transformation of awareness initiated through the

wearing of tefillin moves from mind/intellectual, to heart/emotional, to body/instinctual. On a simple physical level, your hands are tied so they cannot just move around at will. Inwardly, there is the integration of this reality and our hands/instincts are bound to our higher, deeper purpose in being created.

This is the true transformation of the animal within — the natural instincts of the person wearing the tefillin.

TRANSFORMING THE YETZER

Transforming the animal within to something kosher, i.e. "that which is permitted to your mouth," means that not only are our thoughts affected, but even our bodies are transformed.

We are seeking to align our actions and instincts with our feelings and emotions, as well as our thoughts and deepest beliefs. The ultimate end goal is the construction of a consistent and transparent conscious way of being, where what we do is in line with what we feel, which is in line with what we know, which is in line with what we believe.

Wrapping tefillin tames our inner animalistic temptations. The numerical value of the word tefillin is 570: Tof/400, Pei/80, Lamed/30, Yud/10, Nun/50 = 570.

This is the same numerical value of the word *Yetzer Rah*, Negative Inclination. *Yetzer*: Yud/10, Tzadik/90, Reish/200 = 300. *Rah*: Reish/200, Ayin/70 = 270. 300+270=570

The *Yetzer* is not negative, rather it is self-serving, and we, depending on how we express it, make it evil (*Tanchumah. Bereishis*, 7). The Yetzer is our survival instincts programmed into our physical body, as well as our reactive emotions imprinted into our heart. It is who we are on the most basic neurological level. In this regard we are similar to animals and all of creation. The Yetzer acts instinctively and reflexively, seeking to protect and promote its own life and the life of the entire group or species. This is why the yetzer ha'rah is also called the animal soul. It only becomes evil, if we make it evil. If we meekly surrender to our ego-based emotions, the laws of inertia dictate that uncontrolled selfishness will lead to negative behavior. When a totally selfish person needs to eat and does not have the means or the will to properly acquire food, he will think nothing of stealing or threatening another's wellbeing to meet his needs.

Tefillin are meant to mitigate and subdue the influences of our animal soul, our instincts and reactive emotions. Through the act of wrapping tefillin comes a new mindfulness concerning our ability to be able to control ourselves and make better judgments in dealing with our base or bodily instincts.

When you take the Shin as shown on the side of the head tefillin, and combine it with the letter Dalet, which equals 4, from the four compartments within the head tefillin, you get the Hebrew word *Sh'ed*, which literally translates as demon — the energy of the yetzer rah. Through the Yud, which comes from the shape of the *Kesher*, or knot, on the hand Tefillin, we are able to tie down and bind the Shin-Dalet. When the Yud is combined with the Shin-Dalet we get the word Sha-D-Y (Shad-ai), one of G-d's names that means 'Enough' *(Zohar III, 283a)*. So instead of the chaotic energy of Sh-ed pulling us haphazardly in every which direction, we are able to say Enough to those energies and appetites that can throw us off balance. *

Additionally, we can arrive at this same letter combinahtion and teaching by using the knot of the Head Tefillin, which is also shaped as a Dalet, rather than the four compartments. When combined with the Shin from the side of the Head tefillin, we arrive once again at the word sh-ed or 'demon'. We need the Yud from the knot of the hand tefillin to reveal one of the names of Hashem, which serves as the neutralizer of the demonic energies of sh-ed. We can see

---

*In addition, there are nine lines contained within the two Shin's of the head Tefillin: 3 plus the base in one Shin, and 4 plus the base in the other. The number nine in repetition helps break all 'negativity' *(Sefer Chasidim)*. Thus, the nine lines of the Head Tefillin break all shackles of the Shin-Dalet (i.e. demonic, sh-ed) energy *(Ben Yehoyadah*, Berachos, 6a).

from both of these examples that we need to dedicate both our hands/actions as well as our heads/thoughts to Divine service and personal growth. Otherwise, if it's all in our heads or all in our hands, there is only sh-ed, chaos and negativity.

Essentially, the knots of the Tefillin serve to tie down the negative, animalistic forces within and allow us to have clearer vision, better judgment, and a better sense of right and wrong.

As noted, the gematria of the word tefillin is 570. The word *Rasha*, which is an evil person, also equals 570. Rasha: Reish/200, Shin/300, Ayin/70 = 570. So just as the tefillin help to rectify one's Yetzer Rah, the ultimate effect is that the tefillin help us to elevate ourselves from the state of being a Rasha. The act of wrapping the tefillin neutralizes our inner rasha by giving us the opportunity to open up and pass through an inner *Sha'ar,* or gate, in our mind so as to expand and raise our consciousness to a spiritual level.

To further illustrate this, we can see that the word Sha'ar also equals 570. Sha'ar: Shin/300, Ayin/70, Reish/200 = 570. Taken all together we can learn that Tefillin (570) are directed towards the rectification of our Yetzer Rah (570) and inner Rasha (570), and they do this by providing us with a visceral symbolic experience meant to open up a Sha'ar (570) for us to pass through on our path of transformation.

ANIMAL SKINS
THE MATERIAL OF THE MITZVAH

In a very tangible and earthy way, the wrapping of animal skins, the parchment and leather straps, around our own skin ties down the animal within the body, on both a literal and figurative level, effectively evoking the experience of this transformation.

The Torah describes how when Yaakov was living with Lavan, his father in law, the two reached a deal — a sort of severance package — that indicated that when Yaakov, who had been serving as the shepherd of Lavan's flocks, left Lavan's home, all the spotted, streaked, and speckled sheep would belong to Yaakov and all the monochromatic sheep would belong to Lavan.

"Yaakov then took fresh cut branches...and made white stripes on them by peeling the bark and exposing the white inner wood of the branches.... Then he placed the peeled branches in all the watering troughs, so that they would be directly in front of the flocks when they came to drink, and that they [the animals] should conceive when they drank. And the flocks conceived before the rods. And they bore young that were streaked or speckled or spotted" (*Bereishis*, 30:37-39).

This act of placing the striped rods in the waters, says the Zohar, is the way that Yaakov achieved the essential goal of tefillin *(Zohar 1,* 162b). Literally, the placing of these rods, which represented the act of wrapping tefillin, caused a transformation of the actual animals from being monotone to becoming streaked or spotted.

This transformation was also a spiritual elevation for the animal itself, as it were, moving from the ownership of Lavan, the deceiver, and moving into the ownership of Yaakov, the *Tzadik*, the righteous one.

Yet clearly the biggest and most important transformation is within Yaakov himself. At this point in the narrative of Yaakov's life, in his own story, he is at a crossroads. He begins his journey to Lavan's as a simple man, an *Ish Tam*. He is a 'man of the tent', an introvert, reserved and detached from the mundane. He is single, living in his parents home, sheltered from the big world outside the tent. And then, through a series of circumstances and consequences he is forced to leave his fathers home, out into the world, where he will marry, have children, and need to make a living — all things that would appear to be concerns of the external world, animal appetites, and needs of the body.

And so, he journeys from his father's home only to arrive at Lavan's, where he eventually marries, has children, and works to earn a living. But at each juncture his shrewd father in law cheats him out of what is due to him. The peeling and placing of the rods represents a turning point in Yaakov's life, where, because of his own action, he becomes wealthy and independent so he can eventually leave his father-in-law's home to establish a home for himself and his family.

Yaakov's physicality is no longer outside his spirituality, they are integrated; making a living is also a spiritual work. This is the foundation of the nation of Israel, the twelve tribes.

In this story, Yaakov is learning and also showing us how to employ physical objects to project and channel spiritual reality. The first encounter with the 'house of Lavan' was at the well, many years prior, where Yaakov lifts the stone from the well. This is the beginning of his spiritual transformation from the man of the tent to the man of the world, and yet, he is always infusing the ways of the world with the wisdom of the tent. So first he elevates and lifts the stone from the well to reveal the hidden waters — i.e. the deeper/higher wisdom of the Torah. And now the revealed waters, which represent the wisdom of the world itself, is a place to position the symbolic tefillin (i.e. the peeled rods). First he lifts the inanimate, a stone, and now he is dealing with the vegetative, wood, and even deeper, elevating the animal kingdom.

This is an outward manifestation of an inner transformation, projecting and channeling spiritual reality into the physical world.

Today, our own placing and putting on of tefillin, which are literal animal hides, is a very visceral, primordial, and tangible method of harnessing and channeling spiritual reality through animal life. It is a demonstration of the philosophy and practice of elevating the world at large to a state of *Kedusha,* or holiness. First we write the holy wisdom of the Torah on the parchment (animal hide) and then we craft them into a ritual object to fulfill a Mitzvah. They then become in fact, the objects of the Mitzvah. When we wrap ourselves in the animal skins with the sacred writing inscribed on them we are able to feel these ideas very literally in the body, that we are subduing the animal within from that which is "permitted to your mouth" — the skins of kosher animals.

Tefillin are called an *Os,* which literally means a sign. Os is spelled Aleph-Vav-Tof. Aleph is the first letter in the AlephBet, Vav is known as a connecting letter (it literally translates as 'and'), and Tof is the final letter of the AlephBet. So Os can be understood as incorporating everything from Aleph till Tof; from the highest to the lowest, from the beginning to the end. Tefillin is the connection between *Ruchni,* spirituality, and *Gashmi,* physicality, between the Aleph and the Tof.

Tefillin is the link from this world to the upper/inner worlds, it is like an antenna linking us to Transcendence and transforming the world below as we move into the realm beyond.

ANIMAL SKINS
THE MEANING OF THE MATERIAL

Animal skin is the main ingredient used to make Tefillin. Essentially, there is the parchment, the box, and the straps.

Both the parchment and the straps are made from animal skin, yet, there is a difference between them (Alter Rebbe, *Likutei Torah*). The parchment goes through a long and involved process in order to be rendered inscribable, whereas the leather straps are less refined. To create parchment there needs to first be a splitting of the hide. It is then flayed, soaked, and so forth. What this means is that the straps are more connected with the natural animal world than the parchment, which is more processed.

So the inner skin, the parchment, which has words of Torah written upon it, is already farther along the process of being transformed from its natural condition to a more domesticated state. The straps themselves are less tame so to speak, less worked over. They represent and evoke a more visceral, animal sensation; there is still wild energy present. By wrapping our body with the straps of tefillin it is a symbolic way of demonstrating that we are now taming our own animal instincts in order to direct them towards our true purpose and soul reality.

Put another way, the straps represent something that is still in its lower nature but is being elevated, whereas the parchment is already elevated.

To further illustrate this idea of the leather straps representing something low, or unrefined, we can look to an oral tradition that links the tefillin straps to shoes, which function under our bodies, at the lowest possible point.

When our ancestor Avraham did not want to receive any gifts from the condemned city of S'dom he proclaimed that he would not take even, *Me'chut V'ad Sroch Na'al,* "not even a thread nor a leather shoe strap" *(Bereishis,* 14:23). In the merit of his refusal of even a string, we, his descendants, merited to receive the mitzvah of the strings of Tzitzis, and in the merit of his refusal to receive even a leather shoe strap, we merited the leather straps of tefillin *(Sotah,* 17a).

The animal hide straps tie down, as it were, the base animal instincts of the human being.

TRANSFORMING ARROGANCE, DESIRE AND JEALOUSY

There are three principal destructive activities in Torah thought: *Avodah Zarah, Z'nus,* and *Shefichas Damim,* or, idol worship, adultery and murder.

Avodah zarah, idol worship or alienated worship, is primarily a distorted craving of the mind, or the intellectual ego, which seeks to assert that 'I alone am my creator.' This stems from an inflated or exaggerated ego, a function of overwhelming arrogance.

The other two actions — adultery and murder — are rooted in the emotional ego, which craves the fulfillment of lust and revenge. Even when lust or revenge are not carried out to the extremes of adultery or murder, Heaven forbid, their subtler expressions are still discernible and destructive.

Therefore, there are three issues that virtually everyone must contend with:

1)   *Kavod* — the inclination to egoic self-honor or self-worship, otherwise known as inner idol worship,

2)   *Ta'ava* — selfish desire which leads to lust, and

3)   *Kinah* — or jealousy, which leads to revenge and acts of murder, whether figurative or literal.

The Mishna says, "Jealousy, lust, and the pursuit of honor take a person out of the world" (*Avos*, 4:21). These are the three forces of *Choshech* or darkness within: jealously and revenge, selfish desire and lust, ego and self-honor. These three "take a person out of the world", i.e. they do not allow a person to live freely and fully. For truly, all three of these appetites or character traits often lead one down a path of obsession and the feeling of being consumed by them.

Darkness or *Choshech* is also an acronym for *Chamor*, donkey, *Shor*, bull, and *Kelev*, dog *(Tikunei Zohar, Emek HaMelech)*. These three animals also represent jealousy, lust, and honor-seeking.

The donkey is associated with *Yishmael*, whose overabundance of *Chesed* or loving kindness and giving, led to imbalance and acts of lust. The bull is associated with *Eisav*, whose overabundance of *Gevurah*, strength, led to acts of aggression and murder. The dog is associated with *Amalek*, whose overabundance of self importance led to the extreme arrogance of self-idolatry (*Pri Tzadik.* Chanukah 2).

Yaakov was the first person recorded (in the Zohar as mentioned) as having tapped into the energy of tefillin through the placement of the striped bark at the watering hole before Lavan's sheep. The numerical value of the name *Yisrael*, the name Yaakov received from the Angel he wrestled, is 541, which is the same value as the two combined words *Ohr*, light, and *Choshech*, darkness. Through the spiritual qualities of tefillin, he was able to transform darkness into light, physical into spiritual; he transformed his three lower instincts into beneficial energies. This is the inner reason why, when Yaakov was struggling with the angelic spirit of Eisav, the angel became frightened and backed off. It had become aware of Yaakov's tefillin *(Meam Loez,* Ekev).

Yaakov became a master of his instincts. He says before he encounters Eisav: "*Katonti M'kol Ha-chasdim*", "I have been humbled by all Your kindnesses" (*Bereshis,* 32:11). Thus, he was not jealous of his brother, and he did not seek revenge or harm, for he had mastered and transformed his sense of jealousy.

The hand tefillin eradicates the impulse to murder, the aggressive energy of the bull, and the head tefillin serves to eradicate negative desire and lust, the energy of the donkey (*Sheim M'shemuel,* Toldos). Therefore, the hand tefillin is placed on the left hand, the side of gevurah. The straps wrap around and restrain the left arm, thereby taming, subduing and breaking the *kelipa* of the bull and aggression. Eventually, this influence transforms the energy of gevurah into a source of power rather than a tool of force, as explored earlier.

The head tefillin brings wisdom down into the whirlpool of our desires, creating level-headedness, breaking the *kelipah* of the donkey. As the tefillin, sits above us, atop our head like a crown, it is tangibly humbling our ego. We are aware that we are "carrying the seal of the King upon our head."

By putting tefillin on even just once in his life, a person alters the spiritual status of his body, and his *Ohr Makif,* or surrounding light, is forever changed. This ohr makif is something like an energy field, or an aura charging the space of the *Nefesh* dimension of soul. The nefesh extends up to six feet around the body. According to *halachah*, we can acquire an ownerless object by merely being within six feet of the object, since it is within our personal soul-space *(Bava Metziya,* 10a*)*. This projection of energy is our *makif.* The act of putting on tefillin changes the tone of this projection, inclining it toward luminosity, rather than shadow and darkness.

CHAPTER II: REMEZ
BINDING OURSELVES TO OUR BELOVED

CHAPTER II: REMEZ
BINDING OURSELVES TO OUR BELOVED

The intention of tefillin is to bind oursleves to our Beloved. We are commanded/invited to "love Hashem with all our heart". How do we ensure this? By "*[taking] these words which I command you today, [placing] them upon your heart… [and] binding them as an Os, a sign, upon your hand" (Devarim, 6:8)*. Hashem, the Beloved, says to the people of Israel, "*Place me like a seal over your heart, like a seal on your arm" (Shir Hashirim, 8:6)*. With the hand tefillin we place a seal of love upon our arms and our hearts.

Many of the early commentators such as R. Menachem Saruk, Rashi, and the Even Ezra write that the word the Torah uses for tefillin (of the hand) — *Totefos* — originates from a root which means speech, as in "*V'hatef,* speak to the south" *(Yechezkel, 21:2)*. This subtle linguistic connection between tefillin and speech reminds us that when seeing the tefillin we are to be reminded of the Exodus from Egypt and begin to speak of it. We therefore place this seal of love upon our hearts and hands in order to remember that we were, and are still, loved; that Hashem took us out of Egypt, from bondage, and brought us to freedom.

Hashem is our Creator, our King, our Master, Infinite Presence, the awe inspiring and holy fear inducing Transcendent One. But Hashem is also our parent, our friend, and our confidante. Hashem is also our lover and spouse, intimate and extremely close to us. One of the ways the Torah describes our relationship with the Creator is the image of bride and groom — deeply in love and totally committed. Indeed, when approached poetically, the Divine metaphor of the spouse and lover is one of the most exalted and evocative in all the repertoire of Torah symbolism. Hashem is the Groom, and Israel the bride. But not only is the collective body of *Am Yisrael*, the People of Israel, considered to be the bride of the Most High, each one of us individually is also considered to relate to the Holy Groom in this way — our soul is the bride wedded to Hashem, the groom.

This manner of passionate, spiritual, and loving relationship is depicted exquisitely in the book *Shir HaShirim*, the Song of Songs. According to our sages, beneath the surface of such stormy love poetry is actually the most exalted analogy of the love and yearning between a groom and bride, between the Soul of Am Yisrael, and Hashem. In fact, when the Sages debated about whether or not to even include Shir ha Shirim as one of the books of Tanach, considering its overt imagery, the final decision was left to Rabbi Akiva who declared in no uncertain terms that "if the whole Tanach is Holy, then the Song of Songs is the Holy of Holies!"

In our relationship with Hashem we can feel that Hashem is the giver of life, the masculine principle, as it were, be- stowing life from above; and we are the bride, the receiver, the feminine principle, receiving our life here below. When we understand our role as cosmic receiver, we can either choose to focus our awareness on the aspect of Hashem as Ultimate Giver, source of all life, and we are the mere recip- ients of Hashem's light, or we can decide to focus our atten- tion on actively participating in the reception of Hashem's light and love. Then the question becomes more about what we do with the light and blessings, how do we implement and utilize what Hashem has given us?

The head and hand tefillin symbolize and embody these two qualities. The head tefillin, which we wear above our head represents the masculine energy, referred to as *Duchrah*. The hand tefillin, which we wear wrapped around our left- arm all the way down to our hands and against our hearts, is referred to as *Nukvah*, the feminine energy. Therefore, the head tefillin represents the Groom, or the gift and blessing that comes from from Above. In this place we are simply re- ceiving from Above. The hand tefillin represents the Bride, the commitment of the Receiver to be present and productive with that which is received, as well as the active intention to existing in a state of union with the Above.

THE DIFFERENCE BETWEEN BEING AND DOING AS REPRESENTED IN THE TEFILLIN

When the Torah speaks about the tefillin it says, *"You shall bind them as a sign upon your hand, and they shall be for a reminder between your eyes."*

A careful reading of the Torah reveals a slight variation in syntax when referring to either the head or hand tefillin. With regards to the head tefillin it says, it *"shall be"*, and with regards to the hand tefillin it says, *"and you shall bind"*, suggesting that the Mitzvah of the head tefillin is somehow passive — it "shall [just] be"; whereas the Mitzvah of the hand tefillin is conceived of as more active — "you shall bind." Furthermore, as the Rogatchover Gaon writes, the Mitzvah of the head tefillin is continuous, meaning that every moment we are wearing the head tefillin it is considered as if we are performing a new Mitzvah, as it says "And they shall be", which is perpetually in the present tense. Whereas the hand tefillin is more connected to the actual act of binding, as it says, "and you shall bind", implying that once it is tied upon the hand have we fulfilled the obligation *(Tzafnas Paneiach)*.

What's more, there is a debate among *Poskim*, Halachic deciders, with regards to the knot of the head tefillin. Say, for example, a person borrows another person's tefillin and they have a smaller or larger head than them, so they open up and adjust the knot to fit their head. According to the Avnei Nezer, the newly created knot is not a proper knot *(Teshuvos, Orach Chaim,* 183). Since the knot will not last twenty-four hours, its not considered a valid knot. Most Poskim argue and allow this retying and adjusting of the knot. They say that even a knot that holds for an hour or so is considered a good/real knot. Either way, what we see from this is a strong conviction that the knot of the head tefillin needs a sense of permanence.

Contrast the sense of permanence of the head tefillin with the hand tefillin. Regarding the hand tefillin it is almost the opposite. According to one leading opinion, we need to tie, or at least tighten, the knot of the hand tefillin each day from new. It is insufficient to merely have the knot remaining tied or tight from a day ago (*Tosefos*, Menachos, 35b).

Clearly, we can see from these examples that the knot of the head tefillin needs a sense of permanence, whereas the knot of the hand tefillin needs an approach of daily renewal, a retying, or tightening each day anew.

These paradigms can both be understood as referring to attributes and actions of Hashem, which reveal the relational differences between our natures, as well as illuminate the ultimately paradoxical nature of our relationship with Hashem. The head tefillin correspond, as it were, to the aspect of Hashem, which is unchanging — you cannot add or subtract from Infinite Unity, it remains the same before creation, during creation, and after creation. The hand tefillin correspond to Hashem as the Creator in and through time. The Creator sustains creation, and correspondingly — us, through a process of constant and continuous creativity; perpetually renewing the world anew every day, every moment, in deed — right now.

Essentially, there is a higher Kedusha to the head tefillin then the hand tefillin (*Menachos*, 34. *Bach*, O'C, 32). As stated, the head tefillin represent a passive act, but still one that is continually renewed. This means that even though it has the quality of permanence, it is experienced fresh and not stale, suggesting a paradoxical reality that is out of the ordinary and beyond the natural. This dynamic can be compared to the permanance of marriage, matched with the miracle of falling in love again every single day.

This is because the head tefillin represents the Giver, the Creator, or the Permanent. When putting on the head tefillin we are mere passive recipients of Hashem's blessings and abundance, and thus we are merely placing them there. The hand tefillin represents us, the impermanent, that which is being continually recreated. Therefore we tie or tighten the knot of the hand tefillin anew each day.

The head tefillin is placed, the hand tefillin is tied. Hand tefillin is something we do, we work on it, we tie our hands and control our emotions. The head tefillin works on its own, we do not work on it, it works on us. We do not have to tie the head tefillin, we simply place them Above our heads. Indeed, it is similar to a majestic crown of glory that is placed upon us.

THE CROWN OF TEFILLIN

In fact, tefillin is called our crown *(Shulchan Aruch,* O'C, *Beis Yoseph,* 25*).* Tefillin is also called our "turban," or hat, but even deeper, it is also called our "glory"; our hat of glory (*Yechezkel,* 24:17, *Sukka,* 25b). Appropriately, Rabbeinu Asher, the *Rosh,* would place the head tefillin (and hand) and then recite the morning blessing, "Who crowns Israel with glory."

Our tefillin is akin to the crown of Torah. Our sages tell us that tefillin is similar to the *Tzitz,* the head-plate, worn by the *Kohen Gadol* or High Priest. For just as regarding the Tzitz there was a prohibition to have any *Hesech Ha'da'as,* distraction, so too when wearing the tefillin we are obligated to remain focused and aware of this awesome opportunity and responsibility. And furthermore, the name of Hashem is only written on the Tzitz once, so how much more so are we not to have any Hesech Ha'da'as when wearing tefillin which contains numerous mentions of Hashem's name (*Yuma,* 7b-8a). So while the Tzitz is the "crown of *Kehunah*" or priesthood, the tefillin, who's objective is that "the Torah of Hashem may be in your mouth" (*Shemos*, 13:9), is the "crown of Torah", in a quite literal sense. Moreover, if the Tzitz was considered the crown of the Kehunah, and only available to be worn by the priestly class, it is quite a blessing to have a crown that all can wear — tefillin — for we are commanded to be a "nation of priests."

Tefillin is not only the crown of Torah, but more pointedly, tefillin is similar to the crown a bride wears (like a tiara) at her wedding. At the giving of the Torah, Hashem gave us all crowns (*Shabbos*, 88a). Just as a bride receives a crown to wear for her wedding, tefillin is the crown we received on the day of 'our wedding'. Our wedding day is the day of the receiving of the Torah (*Ta'anis*, 26b).

By putting on the head tefillin we are donning our bridal crowns — the crown of glory, the crown of Torah — and by binding ourselves with the hand tefillin we are symbolically tying ourselves, hands and heart, in betrothal to Hashem.

Many have the custom while wrapping the tefillin around their hand to recite the verses in Hoshea (2:21-22), *"I will betroth you unto Me for ever, I will betroth you unto Me in righteousness, and in justice..."*

So we have the head tefillin on, the crown that demonstrates that we are Hashem's bride, and we have bound our arm in the hand tefillin, and then we wrap the straps of the hand tefillin around our finger thereby creating a wedding ring (*Shar Ha'kavanos*, Inyan Tefillin, 5). We are biding ourselves to Hashem forever in holy union.

In addition to the reciting of this verse there is a custom of the wise to kiss the tefillin before and after putting them on (*Avudraham*, from the Geonim. *Shulchan Aruch*, O'C, 28:3). This is a sign of reverence. Yet, the inner purpose is again connected to the relationship between a Bride and Groom. *Neshikin*, the aspect of kissing, is considered a lower level, or preliminary form of *Yichud*, or union. So first there is the lower level, and then the actual act of wrapping the tefillin is the higher, complete, Yichud, the Yichud of 'face to face'.

The same is true in reverse; we slowly and gently leave the embrace of the Yichud by giving the tefillin a kiss as we take them off.

CREATION AS AN ACT OF LOVE, TEFILLIN AS A SIGN OF COMMITMENT

Let us now delve a bit deeper into the bride-groom dynamic in order to understand the idea of Yichud with Hashem.

Hashem is absolute Oneness — the ultimate perfection and unity. And yet, a desire is aroused and emerges from on

High for a relationship; a desire to create 'an other', something outside of the oneness capable of appreciating, knowing, and loving. Hence, the creation of a world of multiplicity, of finite perception, of time and space, of bodies and things, of objects and subjects.

All for the sake of a realtionship, for the purpose of love.

This love is the foundation of creation: A love characterized by a desire to give, to offer what is best of oneself to another who would be able to receive this gift of love.

Hashem, the source of the *Ohr Ein Sof*, the endless light, is seamlessly one. Hashem does not lack, has no imperfection, and is absolutely perfect. And yet a desire to give, share, and create emerged from within this Infinite Unity. In the process of bringing creation into being, Hashem performed the greatest act of love — a supreme contraction and concealment of the Infinite Light's expression.

For without the contracting and withdrawing of the Infinite Light, the finite vessels, the stuff of creation, could never have come into being. In the context of pure infinity, the very existence of a finitude would be superfluous and overwhelmed in the presence of the Infinite. Indeed, the greatest act of love is to stand back, allowing an other to have space to be themselves. The Creator did and continually does exactly this; contracting the Infinite light to allow for the creation – and being – of a finite world to come into focus.

In time, when we, as created, rational, self-consious, finite beings, recognize Hashem's light and the Unity within all of creation, it will be achieved through our own initiative, and our own free choice. This new reality, wherein "G-d will be One and His name will be One," will be, in a manner of speaking, our own creation.

Something just given to us, whether an actual object or an idea, without us having to work on securing it leaves us with an inner sense of shame. We feel inadequete. This form of receiving without working is called the 'bread of shame.' This is when something is merely offered as a gift from Above. But a 'bread' that we have earned through our own hard work and effort is ours to enjoy and we are proud of it. Simply put, one would rather possess a lesser amount earned than a greater amount given (*Medrash. Sifri*, Hazinu). So, by Hashem withdrawing, as it were, from the realm of Creation in order to allow for a physical reality to be created and sustained, Hashem in turn gave us the wonderful ability to respond to life and to make our own choices; seeking and ultimately finding Hashem's unity throughout all of creation.

Hashem's love for us is unconditional and unbridled. From the perspective of the Infinite, there is no time and nothing grows old or jaded. But it is us who need to be constantly reminded of this limitless and unending love. In our world of time and space, if we do not work on relationships, constantly renewing them in the ever-present moment, they become stale, boring, and something of the past. In this way, relationships that began in great passion tend to slowly fade away if they are not continually rekindled. This takes effort and awareness.

Tefillin is a mark of us rekindling our love. As we put on the tefillin we are taking the words, "You shall love your G-d", and binding them as a sign on our hand. In this way we make our love each day anew and bind ourselves to our Beloved so that even from our time-bound perspective, our most intimate relationship is renewed and reinvigorated — a living truth in the moment.

The hand tefillin is bound to the weaker arm. For righties (the majority), that is their left arm, and for lefties, that would be their right arm. The wrapping of this sign on our weaker arm — which is literaly weaker in terms of physical strength, but also symbolically represents a spiritual weakness — expresses a commitment to higher consciousness that permeates our entire being, even those parts of self that seem lacking, or weak, in spiritual strength and resolve.

Once we secure the hand tefillin on our bicep, we then wrap the strap around the forearm seven times. This is a reminder of the seven times the bride encircles her groom, as well as the seven blessings that are recited on behalf of the bride and groom as they stand under the *Chupah*, the marriage canopy.

Finally, the hand Tefillin strap is wrapped three times around the middle finger, resembling a ring in a tripled bond of permanence.

Having bound ourselves to Hashem in love and commitment, we gently place a crown upon our heads, the head tefillin. Situated on top of the skull, 'above the brain', the head tefillin represents a space beyond mind. This is consciousness before differentiation, the deepest cosmic desire, the underlying purpose of all creation, the primal urge to create the space for an other to exist. Through the placing of the head tefillin, we direct our awareness back to that infinite space, the fertile void, in the hope and prayer that in this apparently separate world Hashem's presence should become revealed.

CONNECTING WITH THE NURTURING G-D THROUGH TEFILLIN

"And all the peoples of the earth shall see that the name of Hashem is called upon you'. This refers to the tefillin of the head" (*Berachos*, 6a).

The name of Hashem is upon us as we wear the Tefillin.

One of the Torah's names of G-d is Sha-D-Y. This name is comprised of the three letters: Shin, Dalet and Yud. The name literally means 'enough'. According to the Medrash, the world, as it was being created, was expanding by Divine force into perfection until the Creator said, "Enough, stop!"

The Name Sha-D-Y is related to the measured amount of Divine energy, which is relegated to be expressed in the universe. Sha-D-Y, as in, "*Sh'Dai B'elokus B'olama*" — "for there is sufficient amount of Divine Light in this world." It is the nurturing aspect of the Creator that provides sustenance in such a way that even a suckling, young child gets the perfect, small, enough amount to be satisfied.

Sha-D-Y is both the aspect of Dai, enough, as well as being related to the word *Shadayim*, that which nourishes a young suckling. True nurturing is when you give a child enough, but not more; enough for their need, but not for their greed; neither starving nor spoiling. This requires one to provide what is requested but not in a smothering manner that impedes the child's ability to fend for themselves, discipline their appetites, or be realistic in their expectations. This is all in the hopes that what they do have should not be an aspect of 'shameful bread.' The same process is in fact rooted in the creation narrative, where Hashem, the Infinite One, contracts, holds back, and ceases to express, so to speak, in order to give us the space to develop a sense of independence and exercise our freewill.

Thus Creation begins with a holding back and withdrawal. This is similar to birth, which begins with a contraction.

This is the reason why, in the Torah, the Name (E-L) Sha-D-Y is always associated with blessings for children (Rokeach, *Sodei Raziya*).

Created Perfection is not the purpose of creation. Rather, the inherent goal of creation is so that we, as imperfect vessels — who are broken, shattered, and living from a place of apparent separation or distance from perfection — should use our own capacities and consciousness to help create perfection. Creation is perfection in a state of becoming. Creativity is perfection in process and potential. This is all part of Hashem's love. For in creating us and the world in an imperfect state, Hashem allows finite beings — us — to act in alignment with the ultimate Source of perfection, and seek to create perfection in our own modest way. When we do so, we are able to appreciate what we create, we feel like we have earned it. And in turn, the reward — the spiritual enjoyment and the pleasure we receive — is that of a creator, not merely a receiver. The bread we eat is eaten without shame.

So the Name Sha-D-Y is a name representing the Divine aspect of contraction or withholding in order to nurture us into maturity, wherein we become the mediums or vehicles that allow for the Divine expression. Through our actions or inactions, our conscious choices or unconscious reactions, we express or obscure Hashem's light in the world.

As we mature in life and begin taking more responsibility for our actions, we are able to realize what true nurturing is, how it relates to our relationships, both with our loved ones and with Hashem. And so we put on the tefillin, binding ourselves — from head to heart to hand — with the Name of (E-L) Sha-D-Y:

Shin, *Dalet*, and *Yud*:
Shin on the *bayis* (box) of the Head Tefillin
Dalet in the knot of the Head Tefillin
Yud in the knot of the Hand Tefillin

Taken all together and unified by our bodies and souls in prayer, wrapped in our tefillin, we give breath to the blessings and wisdom of the Name Sha-D-Y.

CHAPTER III: DERUSH
TRANSFORMING SKIN INTO LIGHT & THE POWER OF IMAGINATION

CHAPTER III: DERUSH
TRANSFORMING SKIN INTO LIGHT & THE POWER OF IMAGINATION

A person who puts on tefillin changes the definition of his body forever (See, *Rosh Hashanah*, 17a). Once a person puts on tefillin he becomes a complete person, the tefillin completes him (*Zohar III*, p. 81a). The tefillin make him one, whole, unified — as opposed to scattered, misaligned, and divergent. In a sense, as the tefillin are bound, so do they bind.

The power of the tefillin is such that it transforms the wearer. Let us understand this deeply. How does this work? And how does tefillin achieve a genuine transformation?

We will begin by revisiting the first allusion to tefillin found encoded in the Torah, but this time from the perspective of *Derush*; that is the story of Yaakov and his father in law, Lavan *(Zohar I, 162b)*. Indeed, Yaakov is the first to be mentioned in connection to some version of Tefillin, and Yaakov is forever associated with tefillin in various ways (See *Kaf Hachaim*, 25:2).

In the Torah we read how Yaakov shepherded Lavan's sheep for many years and how he worked hard to make his father in law a wealthy man.

At some point in time, Lavan offered Yaakov a new salary arrangement: Yaakov will take ownership of all the newly born "streaked, speckled and spotted" sheep, and Lavan will own all the non-streaked animals. To ensure his part, and essentially to cheat Yaakov out of what he deserved, Lavan immediately separated the streaked animals and gave them to his sons, telling them to journey a three days journey away from the animals of Yaakov so that the streaked sheep would not cohabit with the non-streaked sheep, and thereby give birth to streaked sheep, which would belong to Yaakov under the new agreement. Yaakov was thus left with only non-streaked animals, all belonging to Lavan. Yet, Yaakov devised a plan:

"And Yaakov took rods from fresh-cut branches...and made white stripes on them by peeling the bark and exposing the white inner wood of the branches.... Then he placed the peeled branches in all the watering troughs, so that they would be directly in front of the flocks when they came to drink, and they should conceive when they drank. And the flocks conceived before the rods. And they bore young that were streaked or speckled or spotted" (*Bereishis*, 30:37-39).

As they conceived while they drank the waters and looked at the rods, they bore young sheep who were streaked, speckled and spotted. By looking at the rods at the time of conception, the white sheep were influenced by the visual stimulus to have offspring that were striped. The contrast of the white bark on the dark sandy bedrock of the watering hole created a contrast between the light and the darker surface of the watering troughs, and the clear water itself served to magnify this contrast.

This act of laying down the rods in the water, says the Zohar, is the way Yaakov achieved the essential goal of the act of tefillin.

This episode in the Torah with Lavan and Yaakov is also an archetypal narrative. Lavan, whose name in Hebrew means white, has the white sheep. And Yaakov, whose name comes from the word *Y'baka*, breakthrough, as in "*Oz Yebaka K'shachar Ohrecha*," "Then your light will break through like dawn" (*Yeshayahu*, 58:8), gets the streaked or spotted sheep. So, in essence, Lavan represents the dichotomous polarity of a monotone consciousness, i.e. black or white, all or nothing. Yaakov represents 'breakthrough' consciousness, which leads to a more integrated or blended awareness, i.e. spotted or streaked. Indeed Yaakov is the embodiment of *Tiferes*, harmony and beauty, the middle column of the Tree of Life, the blending of Chesed, kindness, and Gevurah, strength and restriction.

Interestingly, this kind of breakthrough perspective does not lead to grey, where both polarities lose their definition, but a more organic blending, as is found in the description of creation in Bereshis: *"there was evening and there was morning, one day"* (*Bereshis*, 1:5) . Both sides are left intact, but they are seen from a wider perspective, which reveals that they are both parts of a single whole. This kind of perception, that breaks through and transcends rigid duality, is a hallmark of Yaakov's journey: from wrestling with both mortal and divine, to seeing the angels both ascending and descending the ladder in his dream, to being a man of the tent who also masters the field and the flock.

Yaakov begins his life journey as a 'man of the tent'. He is called an *Ish Tam*, or simple man. He spends all of his youth, even into his adult life, in his parents home, in the 'tent' — a place of Torah, contemplation, and introspection. This is in contrast to his physically powerful brother Eisav, who is called a 'man of the field', outwardly directed with brute physical prowess.

And then, after a series of traumatic events, Yaakov is sent away by his mother, who loves and protects him, to Lavan's home to find a wife, build a family, and begin to make a living on his own.

And this he does. When the story of Yaakov placing the rods in the water hole takes place, he is already married with many children and has proven himself to be quite a successful person of the world. He has built a sizable fortune for his father in law, Lavan, as well as siring and supporting a large family, along with two wives and their two handmaidens.

This outward movement of Yaakov means that he is beginning to elevate the world around him. He is learning how to direct and channel spirituality with and through the material world. On a deeper level, this alludes to the ability to extract and project divinity, purpose, meaning, and morality, from within, as well as into, the chaos and confusion of the world; to elevate the apparent darkness into light. In the context of the story, this elevation is achieved by Yaakov transforming the *Ohr*, skin, of the physical sheep, from Ohr with an *Ayin* (skin), into Ohr with an *Aleph* (light) — transforming their skin into light. Or put another way, empowering their inner light to emerge and break through the surface of their skin.

Shortly after this episode with the sheep Yaakov receives another name. When he battles the angel of Eisav, the spiritual root of the 'man of the field' and is victorious, he demonstrates that he has become a master of his own inner physicality, while at the same time remaining connected to his spiritual nature and roots. After thus proving that he can elevate the darkness of the world and reveal light, having gathered heaps of wealth and cattle and yet remaining a man of virtue, truth and justice, he is given a new name, *Yisrael* or Israel.

The numerical value of the name Yisrael equals 541, the same as the total of the combined words *Ohr*, Light and *Choshech*, Darkness. His name alludes to his ability to strike a harmonic balance between the force of darkness (the ways of the world, of brute physicality) and the force of light (the ways of a spiritual existence, of morality and higher purpose), revealing the ultimate unity between them both. Yisrael is one who is able to master, control, and eventually elevate darkness into light, showing that there is in fact only the Light of Hashem.

One of the symbolisms of the donning of the tefillin, especially wrapping them around our bear arm, is that we are making ourselves striped, as it were, like the sheep in the story. We are creating a contrast between our lighter skin and the jet-black straps of the tefillin, thereby bringing them into greater compatibility.

TEFILLIN, MENORAH, AND THE BEIS HAMIKDASH

The tefillin, especially the head tefillin, resemble the Menorah or Candelabra of the *Beis HaMikdash*, the Temple. The two Shins on the head tefillin — one Shin with three prongs and the other with four, seven in total — correspond to the seven branches of the Menorah *(Zohar III, 274a)*, which in turn correspond to the seven openings of the head: two ears, two eyes, two nostrils and the mouth — this is known as the inner, or embodied, Menorah.

The windows of the Beis HaMikdash had a peculiar feature. Normally, windows are shaped with the wider side on the inside wall and the narrower side on the outside, so that more light shines into the interior. Yet, in the Beis HaMikdash the structure was in reverse — the narrower side was on the inside and the wider side was towards the outside. This is because the light of the Menorah was not to simply light up the chamber within, but it was essentially a spiritual light that shown outward to illuminate the darkness of the world outside the reality of the Beis HaMikdash, and thereby elevate the entire world to its desired perfection.

This is the inner purpose of the head tefillin: "All the peoples of the world shall see that the name of Hashem is called upon you'…this refers to the Head Tefillin (*Berachos*, 6a.)." The Light of the Tefillin illuminates the one who wears it, and they, by extension, shine that light out to the rest of the world, initiating a subtle transformation of the garments, the vessels, or the skin, Ohr with an Ayin, of the world into Light, Ohr with an Aleph.

SKINS OF LIGHT
IN THE GARDEN OF EDEN

We begin this process by taking animal skin and elevating it into vessels of light, shifting our perception from blindly seeing the body as a separate vessel of dense matter concealing the Spirit, to truly seeing the body as light, thereby revealing the spiritual manifest in the physical. When our bodies are completely transformed, from Ohr with an Ayin — skin, to Ohr with an Aleph — light, we are no longer *Iver*, blind, we can properly see and be seen for what and who we truly are.

We are then able to perceive Hashem's presence. Because when our bodies have been elevated to a pre-Tree of Duality reality, the body will be revealed as holy, as a body of Light.

In the Garden of Eden, Adam and Chava, Eve, were bathed in the Primordial light of creation, called the *Ohr Ha'Ganuz,* the hidden light. This is a Light that allowed them "to see from one end of the universe to the other." Their bodies, our sages say, were more brilliant than the light of the sun (*Medrash Rabbah*, Vayikra, 20:2. *Mishlei Rabbah*, at the end. *Tikunei Zohar*, Hakdamah. Note: *Bava Batra*, 58a). They had bodies of *Ohr* — with an Aleph, of light. Being bathed in this Light, and thus having bodies of Light, there was a total transparency, and they were able to see from one end of the world to the other.

There was no external or internal separation. Everything was accessible. There was no delay between an aspiration to manifest a talent or a desire and the actualization. But from our perspective, because we experience external separation, we sense duality and not everything is transparent. And because we experience internal separation, we have a desire to manifest a talent or an idea, and sometimes there is a delay, or even a complete disconnect, between our thoughts and our actions.

After Adam and Chava ate from the Tree of Knowledge — of duality and separation — they needed external garments to cover themselves. Prior to this, as the *Shalah HaKodosh* writes, their bodies themselves were the garments that enclothed their soul. Since they identified primarily with their souls and a state of unity, their interface with reality, their garments, were their bodies. Once they identified with the Tree of Knowledge, duality, and separation, they identified primarily with their bodies. In this state, they needed an additional covering, an interface on top of their bodies, and so, the Torah says "Hashem made garments of *Ohr* — with an Ayin, skins, for the man and for his wife, and clothed them" (*Bereishis*, 3:21). So now, external animal skin is their covering. Yet, in the Torah of Rabbi Meir, it says Garments of *Ohr* — with an Aleph, of light (*Medrash Rabbah*, 20:10). Because now, after eating and identifying with the tree of knowledge, our task is to elevate the external world around us and make it transparent to Hashem's Light.

This is our *Tikkun*, repair or realignment: To become transparent to Hashem's light and to manifest a world with no internal or external separation. Where Hashem's light — the purpose of creation — is revealed, both within ourselves and in the world at large.

The vision of the future is when the *Leviyason*, the Leviathan — a giant mythical water animal created on the fifth day of Creation who rules over all the creatures of the sea — will be killed and from the skin of the Leviyason,

Hashem will construct a *Sukka*, or canopy, to shelter the righteous from the sun *(Bava Basra, 75a.)*. For at that time, the *Ohr*, skin, of this giant serpent will be transformed into *Ohr*, light (Gra, *Sifra Tzniusa*, 1, p. 12b).

TEFILLIN AND HIGHER VISION

In the tefillin, there is the skin of the animal used as parchment to write words of Torah upon, and the skin of the animal used for the *Batim* or boxes. The parchment is refined, processed, smoothed, and white, representing something already in the midst of the process of being transformed from mere skin to light. Whereas the actual *Batim* are more raw and black, representing an earlier stage in transformation. Though it too, of course, is now an object of a Mitzvah and takes on an add luminescence, as in, *"Ner Mitzvah, V'torah Ohr,"* "the mitzvah is the lamp and the light is the Torah" (*Mishlei*, 6:23).

The Torah calls the head tefillin, *Totefos*. The word Totefos is connected with the Aramaic word meaning 'to see', as in a form of vision (*Kesav V'hakabalah*, Devarim, 6:8). The Totefos is placed 'between the eyes', but in actuality, it is placed 'above the eyes', representing an elevated vision, a type of seeing beyond our normal capacity, a third eye view so to speak.

Through the act of tefillin, in the language of Kabbalah, we draw down illumination from the transcendent inner light of the *Metzach*, forehead, of the Primordial Man into and through the orifices of the eyes *(Klach Pishchei Chachmah, 32. Adir Ba'maron).* Which, translated, means that through the act of putting on the head tefillin our vision is cleansed, our perception is unclouded. We can come to see reality as it is truly indented to be, in the space of its Primordial existence, in its perfection and realized purpose. This is known as the rectification of sight through the application of vision.

The head tefillin, situated directly above the eyes, beyond what can be literally seen today, speaks of the vision of the future, a glimpse of the final goal of creation, where the world will be a perfect transparent expression of what it says within the tefillin — The manifestation of Hashem's Light and perfect unity.

FOUR LEVELS OF THE BODY/MIND

Tefillin cause a transformation of the most external aspects of the world around us, taking the skin of animals and making tefillin out of them, thereby transforming that skin into light. Additionally, when we use our body to wear the tefillin, we too transform our skin into light. So by utilizing the natural, physical world for holy purposes, we in turn transform and elevate that matter, resultantly transforming and elevating ourselves.

In the skin of the animal itself there is the outer exterior, the *K'laf,* the part where the hair of the animal grows; and there is the interior, the *Duchsotus*, which faces the flesh of the animal. Tefillin need to be made specifically from the *K'laf (Orach Chaim,* 32:7), the outer part, the most external. As Tefillin have the power to transform even the most external skin into vessels of Light.

Let us delve a little deeper into the aspect of skin, what the skin embodies and represents.

Within the body there are four parts as it were. They are the four vessels of the body, from the most inner to the most outer. They are: the *Atzamos* or Bones, the *Gidin* or Sinews, the *Basar*, Flesh, and the (outer layer of) *Ohr*, Skin.

These four bodily dimensions are a reflection of the four types of *Mochin* or Mind, four forms of intelligence that guide the body. The four types of Mochin are: *Chochmah*, wisdom and intuition, *Binah*, reason and cognition, and the third is *Da'as*, experiential knowledge and awareness. We will speak briefly about these first three before introducing the fourth type of Mochin.

Chochmah is, essentially, the right brain — the creative and intuitive aspects of mind. Binah is more the left brain — deciphering, understanding, and breaking down ideas into comprehensive language. Da'as, or knowledge, is primarily located in the frontal lobes of the brain — it is the executive mind, the part of the brain that chooses, implements and decides. Overall these are the three primary forms of intelligence.

In addition there is the fourth element of the mind, and that is the *Koach Ha'M'damah*, the power of imagination. This fourth form of intelligence is the 'skin' of the mind, the external or most projective form of Mochin.

Atzamos/Bones — *Chochmah*/Wisdom
Gidin/Sinews — *Binah*/Cognition
Basar/Flesh — *Da'as*/Knowledge
Ohr/Skin — *M'damah*/Imagination

The Shin with Three Prongs, the inner mind, corresponds to Chochmah, Binah and Da'as. And the Shin with the Fourth Prongs corresponds to the visionary mind, which is comprised of the above three Mochin, as well as a rectified and integrated Koach Ha'M'damah, the Power of Imagination (*Likutei Halachos*, Tefillin, 5:34).

The power of imagination is the most external capacity of the intellect, the 'skin' of the mind. The higher faculties of mind are a person's wisdom, his understanding, and his awareness. This hierarchy is unrelated to surface conscious vs. deeper unconscious parts of the brain. In that respect, imagination is lodged deeper within a person's psyche then mere intellect. Rather this schematic hierarchy is measured in terms of evolution, what makes us human, the complexity of our thought process. And in this way, first is Chochmah, then Binah, then Da'as, then Dimyon.

Much like the shape of the skin is formed by the flesh, the flesh in turn is formed by the sinews and the bones of the body. Similarly, imagination without wisdom, understanding, and balanced awareness is empty of any true, lasting or constructive form.

THE POSITIVE POWER & POTENTIAL DANGER OF THE IMAGINATION

Imagination without the inner wisdom guiding it is an empty shell, negative and potentially destructive. In other words, there is empty or negative imagination, just the shell, and than there is the fullness of imagination, which is positive, prophetic, and insightful (Rambam, *Moreh Nevuchim*). The prophet is one who has a secure, grounded intellect and yet one with a developed power of *Dimyon (Hosha*, 12:10*)*. But healthy, positive, productive imagination is only possible when it's the skin of the flesh, the outer expression of the inner intelligence. Otherwise, even the most beautiful vision is only skin deep, as it were.

As mentioned previously, our sages teach that the word *Totefos*, the way the Torah refers to the Head Tefillin, is comprised of two words, *Tot* and *Phos* (*Menachos*, 34b, *Sanhedrin* 4b). The Moroccan sage, R. Yaakov Abuchetzira writes that the numerical value of *Phos* is 480, same as the word *Lilis* (Lamed/30, Yud/10, Lamed/30, Yud/10, Tof/400 = 480), And *Tot* comes from the word "וטאטתיה במטאטי השמד" / I will sweep her with the broom of destruction" *(Yeshaya*, 14;23*)* So, the word Totefos implies that with the placement of the head tefillin, we are able to sweep away and subjugate Lilis *(Petuchei Chosom*, Parshas Bo).

But what is Lilis? According to our sages, she is the first wife of Adam, who had a falling out with Adam and left him. She is depicted as an archetypal negative energy that does not seek meaningful relationship in a domesticated environment, nor possessing a desire to have children, but rather, to seduce the wasting of seed.

Chazal speak of one not being alone in the home because of Lilis *(Shabbos,* 151b*),* many sources speak of Lilis as being responsible for, Heaven forbid, the death of infants *(Sefer Ha'Peulos,* 3b, 41.p.140*),* and thus the various *Kameios* or amulets used to protect infants. As mentioned, Lilis is also characterized as the archetypal rebellious partner in terms of intimacy *(Eitz Chayim,* 38:2*),* and maliciously responsible for the wasteful expression of masculine energy. *(Sefer Chareidim,* 63*).*

What does this all mean? What is the connection between all the above teachings? There is a negative and destructive notion that one's actions do not have reactions or repercussions. This leads to a state of mind that is incapable of taking responsibility for one's actions. This gives rise to a self-centered style of freedom with no ties; this leads to one having ultimately no conception of any responsibility to outcome. This is the essence of the energy of Lilis. This is the deep *Kelipa,* shell, of fantasy and false imagination. It is based on ungrounded and nonsensical notions of how freedom looks and functions.

The power of the head tefillin breaks this Kelipa and brings a fuller awareness of how life really works. Tefillin imbue one with a mind-opening, heart-sensitizing, and body-centering awareness that leads to a greater respect for one's own energy expenditures, as well as to the negative or positive effects of one's actions on those nearest and dearest to them.

Negative imagination is called *Dimyan Shav*, false imagination or fantasy. By contrast, positive imagination is guided by *Chochmah*, wisdom, and grounded by a healthy sense of *Binah*, understanding and honest evaluation of reality.

FALSE IMAGINATION AND THE SNAKE IN THE GARDEN OF EDEN

With regards to the Snake, the serpent from the Garden of Eden, it says that the snake was Arum *(Bereishis, 3:1)*. Literally, the word *Arum* means sly, a type of sneakiness *(Berachos, 17a. Rashi)*. The snake, writes the *Sefurna*, had an over active imagination. Over active imagination is one that is not grounded in reality, not formed by Chochmah, Binah, and Da'as. Such imagination leads to lustful desire.

The snake functions in the world of fantasy and indeed, when Adam and Chava do eat from the Tree it says "and their eyes were opened and they saw that they were *Arum*" *(Bereishis, 3:7)*, literally, naked, yet also a clear allusion to the

Arum of the snake. So when they saw, i.e. had a clear vision, they were able to see that they were following their false imagination and pursuing a fantasy.

So how does the Snake in the Garden of Eden convince Chava to eat from the Tree? It inculcates Chava with grandiose visions, telling her that Hashem told her not to eat from that tree, because "Hashem knows that when you eat from it your eyes will be opened, and you will be like god" *(Bereishis, 3:5)*. The snake, i.e. false imagination, attempts to infuse Chava with a pompous and presumptuous vision of self, by telling her that the reason she is told not to eat from the Tree of Knowledge is because if she does eat she will become all-powerful.

The Snake, the over-active imagination, clouds Chava's, and our, true vision of reality. And this voice, the voice of the snake is an 'external' voice, a voice that does not come from deep within, but rather, a voice that comes from outside the self.

The Snake, or the external image and voice of fantasy, distorts Chavah's imagination and instills within her a false image and illusory fantasy. The Snake damages the skin of Adam and Chava, both literally and figuratively. In the Garden of Eden, before the Snake convinced them to eat from the Tree of Knowledge, the skin of Adam and Chava was transparent, like the fingernails we have today *(*Medrash, *Yalkut Shimoni* 15:27. R. Moshe Alshich, *Torahs Moshe,* Bereishis*)*.

They were initially created with a shining, transparent skin *(Targum Yonasan. Medrash, Pirkei Rabbi Eliezer)*. And deeper, figuratively, the snake damaged the imagination, the 'skin of the mind', of Adam and Eve.

In truth, the Snake continues to ruin the imaginations of those who choose to listen to the external voice of fantasy. Therefore, the snake is punished, and punishment is cosmic cause and effect, known as *Midah K'neged Midah* or measure for measure. And so for damaging the skins of Adam and Chava, the snake must shed his skin *(Medrash Rabbah,* Bereishis, *Tikkunei Zohar, 92b)*. In order to do this, the snake must find two smooth stones where he can squeeze himself between them in order to pull off his old skin.

Fantasy and false imagination is the root of all negativity and non-constructive thought, which leads to negative and non-constructive words and actions. To be non-constructive is essentially to be idle — to go nowhere or do nothing. We can learn from this that distorted imagination can lead to 'idle worship' — a type of religiosity or spirituality that only serves to bolster one's ego or insulate one from the realities of the world and of themselves.

Certain images of self and reality, completely devoid and detached from actual reality, are often lodged deep in our subconscious. Many people walk around expressing this false image. They act, speak and think about themselves and their reality from a place of total illusion and fantasy. This is the work of the *Nachash*, the snake.

Complete change and realignment includes transforming our inner world, our thoughts and attitudes. Refining these inner garments is especially important after many years of being bombarded with unhealthy images and messages from the popular culture and mass media surrounding us, whether through explicit or subliminal imagery. Over time, this imagery accumulates in the storehouse of our subconscious mind. Certain experiences can trigger this imagery and bring it up into conscious awareness like a belch. To transform ourselves completely we need to work on ourselves from the inside out. We need to learn how to reprogram our imagination, so that it comes from within, from the inside of our balanced mind, and then projects outwards, rather than the other way around.

Healthy imagination is only possible when the skin is the skin of the flesh, of the sinews, of the bones, and deeper, of the *Mochin* or mind. Which means that, when our outer mind, our imagination, is aligned with our inner understanding, wisdom, and experience, then we can be assured that our visions and desires for manifesting in the world are organically authentic, and not externally implanted within us. When there is this alignment than our imagination is redeemed, and there is an elevation of the imagination. Then we can truly say that we are transparent again, our outer is an honest reflection of our inner — in fact, they are one.

The Zohar teaches that the gate of *Kedusha*, holiness, is through the power of imagination *(Zohar I, p. 103b)*. A rectified, redeemed, realigned, properly engaged, and guided power of imagination is holy and noble.

The Chassidic thinker, Reb Tzadok of Lublin, calls the early period of our history — from Avraham until the destruction of the Second Temple — the 'action' period. This period was characterized by the bringing of physical offerings as a way of transforming ourselves and absolving misdeeds.

After the second Temple period until today, our main modality has been prayer and study — i.e. text, speech, and words. Prayer takes the place of the offerings. The coming Redemption, however, is connected with the garment of thought — image and imagination.

Our collective *Galus*, exile, is the alienation of the power of *Dimyon*, or imagination. Our collective redemption is connected with our redeemed imagination. A redeemed imagination is when it is the 'skin of the flesh', it is the outer expression of the balanced and grounded inner thoughts and wisdom. This means that one's imagination is connected to the rest of one's being, it is an extension and expression of their deepest self. False imagination or damaging fantasies occur when we separate our imaginal world from the rest of our being and higher intention.

Interestingly, the Hebrew word for Snake, *Nachash*, has the same *Gematria*, or numeric equivalent, as the word

Mashiach, the redeemer: 358. This is a hint that the ultimate redemption of the world requires the transformation of the *Nachash*, the Snake, into the *Mashiach* — turning false fantasy into holy *Dimyon* or imagination.

One definition of a *Chasid*, a pious individual, is one who maintains control over their minds. This includes, among other things, the power to visualize events or occurrences clearly, for example — the Giving of the Torah or the Holy Temple (*Kuzari*, Ma'amar 3:5). A *Tzadik*, or perfected and fully-realized person, one who is a master of his reality, is someone who has the ability to visualize holy things in his mind as vividly as if they were real *(Sichas Musar, 26)*.

A Tzadik is one who has transformed, or revealed, the innate conditioning of their consciousness. They are no longer slave to the mentalities and thought processes that they received unconsciously while growing up. They have rewired their circuit board, so to speak. And through this process they have enabled their imagination to flow from the inside-out, rather than just chasing after that which is externally validated. In this state of mind, one chooses the contents and functions of the imagination, not the other way around — that would be mere fantasy. The ideal movement is from *Chochmah*, wisdom, to *Binah*, understating, to *Da'as*, awareness, to *Dimyon*, imagination. The skin is formed by the flesh, the flesh is formed by the sinews, and they, in turn, are formed by the bones.

The skin we have today, which is the skin affected by the Snake and damaged by negative imagination, is appropriately called *Mishcha D'Chivya*, garments of the Snake. We strive to realign our consciousness, as before in our primordial state or as a Tzadik with perfect imagination, in such a way that our skin is returned to its original transparency, to be skin of Ohr, with an Aleph, or Light. Skin of light is a perfect reflection of what is going on internally, within the mind. This skin of Light was experienced clearly with Moshe. When Moshe came down from the Mountain his face was radiant *(Shemos,* 34:29*)*. The skin of his face was similar to the skin of Light that Adam and Chavah had before the episode with the Snake and the Tree of Knowledge and Duality (*Rabbeinu Bachya,* Bereishis, 3:21). His Ohr — with an Ayin, skin, was shining, it was transformed into Ohr — with an Aleph, Light.

The transformation of Moshe's skin into light is associated with the Light of tefillin *(Likutei Halachos,* Tefillin, 5:36). Through the Mitzvah of wearing tefillin, we too have access to such a powerful and primordial illumination, depending on how deep we are able to enter into the experience and open ourselves up to receive this light.

Moshe, the greatest of all prophets, is one who had achieved a perfected mind — which is an honest assessment of reality as it truly is — and a perfected imagination — which is the ability to imagine how it could be in potential. Moshe had a perfect mind, which is why he is the perfect teacher of Torah, our ideal Rebbe. He is called *Moshe Rabbeinu*, Moshe our teacher, and he is also the perfect prophet, attaining the highest level of prophecy, direct experience, and being the instrument to take us out of Egypt and slavery. Being a person with a totally transformed and elevated imagination, his outer extremities, i.e. his skin, shined with a brilliant Light and became transparent.

All human beings have the potential to actualize these four faculties of mind. To be fully human, to be a master of your experience, is for the thought process to move from Chochmah to Binah to Da'as, which then inform your imagination as the most external expression. The movement is from the inner to the outer, and thus, you are in control of your imagination, even your dreams are in your control. This is a state referred to as lucid dreaming, where one can consciously act or influence their dream world. To be awake within the dream, rather than to be dreaming while awake, this is the consciousness we are striving for.

For a Tzadik, a totally aligned individual whose imagination is directed and illuminated by the inner resources of their mind — to whom imagination is like the perfect skin of the flesh — such a person has full control over their thoughts. So much so, writes R. Avraham the son of the Rambam, that if such a person has an unusual or unexpected dream, being that they have such control over their imagination and thus their normal dreams, they can generally assume it is a prophetic dream *(HaMaspik L'ovdeh Hashem)*.

False, empty imagination is considered a form of animal/instinctual consciousness, where a person is merely responding to external stimulus out of an unconscious reflex of reactive emotions. A person insults you, and you flare up in anger. The movement is from the outside–in. That person has little to no control over their thoughts, word, and actions.

By taking the skin of the animal, forming the tefillin from this skin, and inscribing the words of Divine Intelligence into it — the portions of the Torah that speak of tefillin on the parchment made out of skin — this is symbolic of our ultimate transformation. The regular practice of wrapping tefillin facilitates the purification and re-alignment of our imagination.

TEFILLIN AND THE EXODUS FROM EGYPT

The Targum Yonasan writes that as the children of Israel left Egypt, being redeemed from both external and internal slavery, they fashioned their tefillin from the skin of the *Korban Pesach* — from the hides of the animal offering of Pesach. The skin of the *Korban* was used to create their tefillin.

The Korban Pesach was their ticket, as it were, to freedom. The Medrash explains that it was necessary for us to perform the Mitzvah of the Korban Pesach (and the *Bris*, circumcision) before we could be redeemed from Egypt (*Rashi, Shemos*, 12:6).

In a way, the skin of the Korban, which became their tefillin, represents the Israelites' redeemed imagination. To further explore this concept we will use another Mitzvah given right around the time of our liberation from bondage in Egypt: The Mitzvah of sanctifying the new month (*Shemos*, 12:1-2).

The very first instruction the Israelites received from Hashem was the Mitzvah to sanctify the new month. In the Hebrew calendar, months are defined by the orbit of the moon, the lunar cycle, while years are determined by the seasonal solar cycle.

The moon waxes and wanes, changing its shape as it moves through its cycle, whereas the sun always appears to be full, so to speak, its shape does not change. As the book of *Koheles* says, "*Ein Chadash Tachas Ha'shemesh*", "there is nothing new under the sun" (1:9). Yet, as the Zohar appropriately adds, under the sun there is no newness, but the moon is constantly changing and new *(Zohar I. p. 123b)*.

A month, which is determined from the lunar cycle, is called a *Chodesh*. Chodesh comes from the word *Chidush*, or new. A year, rooted in the solar seasonal cycle, is called *Shana*, from the word *Yashan*, old.

One's rectified imagination — the ability to not allow reality how it is objectively observed to devastatingly cloud out one's deeper, poetic vision of what could be — is rooted in the fact that creation is continuous. This is understood as the constant renewal of creation at every moment, the *Koach Hischadshus*. And within the cycles of time, this reality of renewal is most overtly and symbolically represented by the lunar cycle.

To become a free people, we first needed to imagine at least the possibility of freedom. We were slaves for so long that we started believing it was the only possible reality, that this was just our lot, that slavery was ontological, inevitable. Hashem wanted us to believe in the miraculous, that it was possible for us to be free. Hashem wanted us to deeply understand that, in truth, nothing is really routine, old, predictable, or even natural. Every moment is a completely renewed creation, a miracle, a novelty. Nature is nothing but a continuously renewed miracle.

To demonstrate this total transformation of the 'skin' of the mind into the creative, positive, productive light of the imagination, the Israelites used the skin of the Korban Pesach for their tefillin. Symbolizing that, in the act of leaving of Egypt, there was a total purification and redemption of the imagination.

Animal consciousness, without Mochin, or mind, is reactive. It is essentially a product of thinking from the outside-in, with external stimuli creating internal reality. What the Torah seeks to create is a process of thinking from the inside-out; from the 'bones of the mind' outward, i.e. from wisdom, to understanding, to awareness, to imagination. Putting on tefillin elevates the animal, both literally, by taking the skins of an animal and using them for a Mitzvah, and figuratively, by elevating and purifying the animal within us. Transforming the negative, empty power of false imagination and fantasy into the fertile vision of prophecy and truth.

USING THE IMAGE TO AFFECT THE IMAGINATION

Returning to the Yaakov narrative, where he places the striped bark at the watering hole, and through that act channels the essence of tefillin. The power of the stripes carved into the bark reflecting in the mirror of the water is akin to the power of imagination upon our internal reality. If we look at or focus on a specific pattern, observing on the outside a certain color or geometric form, this imprints itself upon our internal reality.

Something seen during conception, for example, at the moment of creation, can have a spiritually formative effect and influence the developing fetus. The Medrash mentions the story of a dark skinned king and dark skinned queen who gave birth to a lighter skinned child. Rabbi Akiva suggested that during conception the queen was gazing upon their lighter skinned statue *(Tanchumah,* Naso*)*. The Ramban speaks at length of the power of vision upon us, especially at the time of conception, and the need to be surrounded by holy images, especially at the time of conception *(Igeres Kodesh)*.

When Yaakov placed dark bark with white stripes in the water, the sheep that were looking in the water, saw the white stripes while conceiving, and their thoughts imprinted themselves upon their internal reality, and as such, the sheep they conceived were born striped, streaked and speckled with white.

If we choose the imagery that surrounds us, surrounding ourselves with positive and holy imagery, than our subconscious dreams and self-images will also be productive, holy, and noble. The reverse is also true. By choosing the visuals we surround ourselves with, our imagination will come more under our conscious control, and it will in turn become that much more holy and productive.

Deeper still, this action by Yaakov is much more profound than the sheep merely looking outward at the white stripes and the resultant visual, in turn, effecting them inwardly. For when they observed the exposed bark in the water they saw their own reflection as well. When they drank from the waters, looking down at the bark, they saw their own reflection, and their reflection, the image in the water that they saw, was of a striped sheep. They saw themselves, when conceiving, in the image of a striped sheep. What they saw was not merely striped bark, but in fact, they saw that they were themselves striped.

They became and embodied what they imagined themselves to be. They saw themselves as striped, and so, the children that came from them were striped, because that is the way they saw themselves. Yaakov made the sheep think of themselves — through the strategic use of the visual imagery, the mirror image they saw in the water — as striped sheep.

Tefillin too have this power. Tefillin harness our power of imagination in a positive way. Not only do the tefillin represent the quality of a redeemed 'skin' — imagination — and elevated animal consciousness. But by wearing tefillin we see ourselves as a G-dly people. Imagine yourself as a holy, noble person, and thus give birth to that reality. Imagine oneself a Tzadik, and thus become one.

When we wear tefillin we see ourselves as worthy of wearing Hashem's name and crown on our heads.

Here is a fascinating teaching from the Zohar: The Zohar teaches, *"A person wakes up in the morning, recites a few blessings, puts the tefillin upon his head between the eyes. When he wishes to lift his head, he sees the holy supernal name of Hashem (the 4 compartments correspond to the Four letters in the Name of Hashem — Yud-Hei-Vav-Hei) tied to and imprinted upon his head. He sees the straps hanging from this side and that side near his heart. He is indeed looking at the splendor of the King. He wishes to move his (right) hand, and he immediately notices his other hand tied in the knot of the Holy Name (the 4 portions*

in the hand Tefillin correspond to the four letters in the Name
Ado-nai); whereupon he returns his hand (from doing anything
negative), since he looked upon the Splendor of the King"
(Zohar III, p, 175b).

In simple words, wearing the tefillin on the body transforms — via the visual — the way we look upon our own
bodies, and furthermore, upon our whole self. Seeing ourselves in tefillin, our bodies are forever changed, as they are
now seen as a vehicle that carries the Name of Hashem.

It is a powerful image. First you see yourself adorned in
the Kings ornaments and then you act in a way that is de-
serving of such an opportunity. In this way, when we wear
tefillin, we wear the crown of the King and therefore act roy-
ally.

By choosing to put on tefillin, we are, in essence, using
our conscious mind to effect our subconscious imagination.
It is a deliberate and conscious act. In fact, a child who does
not possess an appropriately mature intelligence should not
put on tefillin. This is intended to be an inside-out choice,
not something imposed from without.

By adorning ourselves with the Seal of The King, *(Akeidas
Yitzchak, 90)*, we start imagining and thinking about ourselves
differently. We realize that we are, in fact, the children of
The King and we begin acting this way. We start living up
to the image we imagine ourselves to be, and who in fact,
we truly are.

CHAPTER IV: SOD

DRAWING DOWN MOCHIN INTO MIDOS AND MA'ASIM

CHAPTER IV: SOD
DRAWING DOWN MOCHIN
INTO MIDOS AND MA'ASIM

Through the act of putting on Tefillin we raise our spiritual consciousness, and more specifically we gain a new sense of *Mochin*, or expanded mind and intelligence.

This idea is reflected in the actual word tefillin. The *Arbarbanel* writes that the word used in the Torah for head tefillin, *Totefos*, is perhaps related to an Egyptian word that means mind.

Verily, as just explored, tefillin are made from animal hide, and yet, to create the more refined parchment we need human involvement. The final product is a combinahtion of human creativity and animal/primal energy. Symbolically, it is our evolutionary ability to transform our unconscious instincts and emotions, *Midos*, into a more mindful, *Mochin*, state of awareness.

Through tefillin we drawn down and access the sixth sense — otherwise known as the 'minds eye' — a higher, deeper vision and mindset. The Torah says we shall place the head tefillin "between our eyes". In truth, we do not actually place them directly between the eyes, but rather on the top of the head, directly above the space between the eyes. This placement represents a drawing down of awareness from the higher mind, from *Keser* or the Crown, the source of spiritual intuition, as opposed to hard-wired animal intuition.

This Light of higher vision is revealed through the tefillin and emanates in such a way that, *"All the peoples of the world shall see that the name of G-d is called upon you."* This level of awareness, this higher mind, moves downward into the body, the gut, or the *kishkes*. The straps of the head tefillin cascade down from the top of the head, the 'mind's eye', laying upon the heart, the emotions, and dangling — according to the very early sources (*Shulchan Aruch HaRav*, Siman 27:20) — till the area of the digestive system in the body, until the *Tabur*, or navel (*Rambam*, H'T, 3:12).

The navel is a remnant of the umbilical cord, where life began in the womb. So the movement of consciousness goes from the mind, the upper part of the body, all the way down to the lower part of the body, all the way back to the beginning of life, thus creating a circuit, as such, from the highest to the lowest dimensions of self. Thus the regular practice of putting on tefillin can help us establish a psycho-physical feedback loop that serves to further us on the path of the ultimate objective, to live through and with Mochin, to draw down cosmic mind and revealed purpose to all of our life and to all of creation.

There is also an opinion that while the left strap should hang down until the Tabur, the right strap should hang until the *Milah*, the procreative organ (*Tur*, O'C, 27). So with this alignment, the circuit is even more inclusive, becoming a spiral rather than just a circle feeding back into one's own life, taking one beyond the womb to the point of one's own creative potential, and into the next phase of the generational journey.

The general movement outlined above is one that goes from the higher sense — the third eye of deeper vision, clarity of mind, and cleansed perception — into, penetrating and influencing, the rest of the body. The five senses — sight, hearing, taste, smell, and touch — are the doors that open into our bodies. What we allow into these doors — what we allow ourselves to see, hear, smell, taste and touch — informs and shapes us. And so, we place the head tefillin, like a crown, on top of the head, the seat of the four senses — sight, smell, taste, and hearing — and wrap the hand tefillin around our arm all the way down to our fingers, representing the sense of touch (*Gra, Agados*, Berachos 1); showing that the head tefillin, with its 'future vision' of deeper insight and clarity, is truly the ruler and internal compass that guides us, while the tefillin of the hand binds our actions and emotions to this higher vision.

Through the laying of tefillin, with the power invested by the Commander of the Mitzvah, we draw down Mochin — big mind and clarity — into our world and our self.

The entire Torah is compared to tefillin *(Makkos,* 11a*).* Tefillin draw down the ultimate wisdom that comes from before creation, the Torah itself. Thus, there are five scrolls in the tefillin, the four individual scrolls in the head tefillin and the one scroll in the hand tefillin, which correspond to the five books of the Torah. The four individual scrolls correspond to the first four books and the single scroll corresponds to the final book of the Torah, which is a 'synopsis' of the other books *(Sefas Emes, Bo).* With the donning of the tefillin we are able to draw down the ultimate Mochin, a sense of clarity and revealed purpose, to our lives and, by extension, the world around us.

SPIRITUAL PROPERTIES OF THE PHYSICAL TEFILLIN

It has been suggested that the actual boxes of the tefillin and their corresponding straps, tied tight around the crown of the head and wrapped on the arm and around the hand, are in fact all placed — by Divine design — on the various acupressure points of the body that activate and stimulate remembrance, calm the mind, and release the self from emotional stress. While this is a creative and fascinating idea, and surely one with some potential merit (if it can be verified), we must not limit the effect of the tefillin upon our whole system to a mere physical sensation, nor should we confine the intentions of He Who Commanded us to wear the tefillin in the first place. For surely, the Creator's design and reasoning is far deeper and subtler than we can even pretend to imagine.

That is not to say that the tefillin are not in fact placed upon a series of key acupressure points along our body's meridians, nor is it to imply that acupressure is not a serious and healing art and science. But ultimately, whether this is accurate and empirical science or not is not entirely the point. For, even if it is verifiable and the boxes of tefillin are in fact resting along actual energetic meridians, this phenomenon is still only a by-product — an outer manifestation of an internal process — that is facilitated and activated by the laying on of the tefillin. For every spiritual truth is manifest in the physical as well. And there is much more to the effect and essence of tefillin than such a reductionist perspective allows.

That being said, now lets explore some deeper teachings of the Torah, to understand a bit about the deeper structure of the tefillin.

There are two tefillins: the head tefillin and the hand tefillin. Each of the tefillin is comprised of a *Bayis* (pl. *batim*), a box or house. Within the box resides the parchment, and upon the parchments are inscribed four chapters from the Torah.

The head tefillin is comprised of four separate compartments containing four separate scrolls, each with one chapter. The hand tefillin is a single compartment with all four chapters on one scroll. Straps hang from the boxes, one which encircles the head and the other that is bound to the arm.

The physical tefillin describe a deeper spiritual reality. The box encircles or houses the parchment. The parchment, in turn, surrounds the black ink of the holy letters.

Essentially, tefillin are three levels deep: The outer two levels are *Makifim*, surrounding forces. The outermost container, the Bayis, or the home, is a *Makif Ha'rachok*, a distant surrounding, as a home surrounds the person dwelling within. The parchment encompassing the letters is also a *Makif*, albeit a *Makif Ha'karov*, an intimate sourunding, in close proximity to the letters, as clothes that garb the wearer. The actual script is Torah itself. It is Divine intellect, internal truth, a *Penimi*, an inward reality.

The boxes, made from the skin of an animal, the same material as the parchment that the words of Torah will be written upon, is also a form of *Mochin*, or intelligence. Yet it one which is still on a level of *Mochin D'katnus*, small or constricted mind, whereas the parchement is *Mochin D'-gadlus*, or big, expansive mind (*Shar Ha'kavanos*, Inyan Tefillin, 4).

So even though the boxes are a Makif, in essence they are lower than the parchment and certainly lower than the actual words of the Torah written upon that parchment. The words of Torah written within the tefillin draw down an overflow of Mochin, and since there is a gushing forth of Mochin, that Mochin spills outwards, as it were, bursts forth and becomes the box of tefillin on the front of the head. The box is the Mochin manifest outwardly. In addition, the *Achurayim* or back side of the overflow of Mochin trickles down and becomes the *Kesher*, the knot, at the back of the head tefillin. So in the front, the bursting forth of Mochin is the actual box of the tefillin, and in the back, the bursting forth of Mochin is manifest in the *Achurayim*, the knot. This knot is the Achurayim of Mochin, the level of 'Leah'.

TRANSFORMING THOUGHT, SPEECH, & ACTION WITH TEFILLIN

The boxes that house the scrolls of the tefillin represent the world of Action. The scrolls themselves represent the world of Speech. The Divine Names written within the scrolls, which need extra intention and Kavanah when written, represent the world of Thought.

These three Garments of the soul also correspond to the three levels of the Soul: Nefesh/Action, Ruach/Speech, and Neshamah/Thought.

And so, with this in mind, we can understand that through the putting on of the tefillin, we are able to transform our thoughts, words, and actions.

To further illustrate this concept, we can add yet another layer of meaning to the matrix created — the three names of G-d encoded within the construction of the tefillin themselves.

There are four compartments in the box of the head tefillin. These correspond to the four letters of the outer-Name, the name we pronounce as *Ado-nai* (Aleph, Dalet, Nun, Yud).

There are four portions of Torah written on the four parchments and placed in the box of the head tefillin. These four portions and parchments correspond to the inner Name, the name we do not pronounce, *Hashem* (Yud-Hei-Vav-Hei).

The name of Hashem is written 21 times within the tefillin. These correspond to the 'prophetic and liberatory' Name, revealed to Moshe at the burning bush, *Ehe-yeh* (Aleph-Hei-Yud-Hei), which numerically equals 21.

These three physical aspects of the tefillin, which correspond to the three levels of our soul, as well as the three Garments of Soul (as mentioned), also correspond to the three

Divine names encoded into the construction of the tefillin themselves.

1. Batim — Ado-nai — Action —Nefesh
2. Parchment — Hashem — Speech — Ruach
3. Divine Names — Ehe-yeh — Thought — Neshamah

THE SEFIROS AND TEFILLIN

The ten *Sefiros*, the emanations through which divine energy flows into the world, emerge in order: the three levels of intellect, down to the seven emotional attributes.

1. *Chochmah* — wisdom or intuition
2. *Binah* — understanding or cognition
3. *Da'as* — knowledge or awareness

These three are collectively called *Mochin*, mind, or *Seichel*, intellect. These — hopefully — guide the seven emotions:

1. *Chesed* – kindness and giving
2. *Gevurah* – strength and restraint
3. *Tiferes* – harmony and compassion
4. *Netzach* – ambition and striving
5. *Hod* – devotion and acknowledgement
6. *Yesod* – connection and relationship
7. *Malchus* –receptiveness and form

Beyond the intellect is Keser, the crown, which represents the deepest desire and divine will of Hashem, as well as within one's very being. The order of the ten Sefiros is replicated ad infinitum throughout every level of the chain of creation: *Malchus* of a higher reality becomes the Keser, the crown, of the next lower one. Keser links the present above with the higher below. So too, within Keser itself there is a level which is drawn downward, called *Arich Anpin* or the long face, and a higher aspect of Keser is connected upward, the final level of the higher world. This higher aspect of Keser is called *Atik*, indicating something that is detached, old and removed.

The *Bayis,* or house, of the head tefillin, symbolizes that most transcendent Makif, or surounding force, the loftiest, most penentrating desire. It crowns and surrounds the head. It represents the deisre and purpose of creation.

From the Bayis, a flow descends into the parchment, and then into the written word, the divine intelligence of Torah. The boxes are traditionally dyed black because it represents the darkest level, beyond comprehension, which is called the 'light of darkness'. It is said about the Most High that, "to You, darkness is light".

The *Batim* contain chapters of Torah that represent intellect — *Chochmah*, *Binah* and *Da'as*. These chapters instruct and guide us on how to live our individual lives and how to pursue our collective purpose.

On each side of the head tefillin is inscribed the letter *Shin*, one with three arms and the other with four. The letter *Shin* itself alludes to *Seichel*, or intellect, and the three arms resprsent *Chochmah*, *Binah* and *Da'as*. First, a thought comes to mind, *Chochmah*. Then, with the faculty of cognition, *Binah*, we comprehend and decipher the thought. Finally, we use our knowledge, *Da'as* to implement our understanding.

Da'as affords us the ability to distinguish and make choices. It ensures that whatever we understand intellectually does not remain purely abstract. Rather, it influences our emotions and informs our behavior. Since choice emerges from Da'as, it is subdivided into a right-sided quality, *Chesed*, love and giving, and a left-sided one, *Gevurah*, strength and restraint.

Being that choices occur in Da'as, and Da'as itself is divided into a right-side and left-side qaulity, the three levels within Mochin are actually four. And so, the head tefillin also bears a four-pronged *Shin*, representing this more detailed understanding of *Seichel*, as well as four divisions within the Bayis.

This division of three and four also coresponds to the division of the three patriarchts — Avraham, Yitzchak and Yaakov — who in turn correspond to Chochmah, Binah and Da'as, and the four matriarchs, Sarah, Rivkah, Rochel and Leah. Since Da'as divides itself into two, Yaakov married two wives: Rochel, the embodiment of Chesed, and Leah, the embodiment of Gevurah.

In Cosmic terms, Keser is the ultimate desire and purpose, the root reason why creation occurred and continues to occur, and Mochin is the blue print, the intellectual framework of how and what to create. But it is only through the lower seven emotional Sefiros that creation actually occurs.

This process is much like our own creative process. We first have a desire, for example to build a home. Then we think of how we are going to create that home, we come up with and draw out the plans. Then we actually create the home. Indeed, the seven-day cycle of creation reflects the seven emotional emanations, with each day representing another Sefirah; Sunday — Chesed, Monday — Gevurah, and so forth.

And so it is in our own lives. Our reality is primarily emotionally based, and the way most people live life is reactive, reflecting their often-unconscious emotional responses to external circumstances and stimulus. It is rare to find clarity of thought, expansive thinking, and openness of mind. Rarely does one experience life driven solely by a crystallized clarity of thought. This is because the Ultimate Keser or inner purpose and the mature deliberation of Mochin, the plan, so to speak, is beyond this world. Our world of the seven-day weekly cycle is primarily an emotional place, a reflection of the seven emotional Sefiros. Keser and Mochin are beyond this world. Our purpose, and the means and ways to attain it, does not always seem so apparent; it needs to be revealed to us.

Since there is a concealment of Keser — the divine desire, the 'why' of Hashem's creation — even the greatest of Tzadikim do not know for certain the distinct purpose of their creation. The Baal Shem Tov said on the day he passed away, "I know [only] now why I was created" *(Igra D'kalah, Vayelech)*. The act of putting on tefillin is intended to open us up so that we may access the hidden knowledge of Hashem's specific desire for us and for our lives. The point of putting on tefillin is to draw down Keser and Mochin into ourselves until the truth of this higher revealed reality infuses our way of being and doing.

FOUR-FOLD REALITY

The idea of drawing down Mochin can also help explain why tefillin need to be square *(Menachos, 35a)*.* The tefillin embody the four levels of Mochin and the four portions of the Torah. These two sets of four both correspond to the four letters in the name of Hashem, the Yud-Hei and Vav-Hei, and to the four sides of a square. *

There are four Torah portions in the tefillin. The portion known as *Kadosh*, holy, corresponds to the first letter, the Yud, the level of Chochmah. This is why this portion speaks of the sanctification of the first born. The portion of *V'haya*

Ki Yiviacha coresponds to the upper *Hei*, the level of *Binah*. The word *V'haya* implies a sense of joy. And joy is connected to the comprehension of Binah. The portion of *Shema*, which speaks of the act of loving G-d "with all your heart", coresponds to the letter *Vav*, the level of *Midos* or emotions. And the portion of *V'haya Im Shamoa*, which speaks about the keeping of the Mitzvos, coresponds to the final *Hei*, the level of *Malchus*, the world of action.

These four letters of the Name of Hashem, which are reflected in the four portions, represent the immanence of Transcendence. Hashem (י-ה-ו-ה) represents the Infinite

---

*NOTE: According to another Kabbalistic source *(the Magid of Kasnitz)*, there is an additional reason why the tefillin need to be square. Tefillin represent the garments of the soul. We are, through the act of laying tefillin, thereby transforming the garments of our body, even the 'skin' as explored earlier, meaning that we are affecting the aspect of Creation rooted in Olam Ha'Malbush, the 'world of the Garment', which is a reality that exists even prior to the first Tzimtzum or 'cosmic contraction'. Olam Ha'malbush is the 'potential to reveal'. This Cosmic Garment is woven from the 231 letter combinahtions, going backward and forward through the AlephBeis — the supernal source of all sounds and vibrations, which are the potential of revealing and creating. After the initial movement to 'potential' to reveal, there was another movement, to reveal from mere 'potential' to' actual Infinity', which 'actual Infinity possesses the 'potential' to reveal Finitude. This stage, from potential Infinity to actual infinity, which in turn contains the potential for finite realty, is called the "folding of the garment". Folding reveals edges, the potential of Finitude. This movement is also referred to as the 'Tzimtzum of the Square', in contrast to the 'later', 'first Tzimtzum' which is the 'Tzimtzum of the Circle'. This is another reason why tefillin need to be square.

---

aspect of the Creator. The four letters that comprise this Name, when rearranged, can spell the Hebrew words for past (ה–י–ה), present (ה–ו–ה), and future (י–ה–י–ה), indicating that this name transcends all concepts of time and movement.

Our reality is one of time and space. Yet, before the creation of space there needs to be 'a before' — meaning, the creation of time. So the *Seder Zeman*, order of time, is the first thing created. Time, and even deeper, the concept of time, is thus the first creation. It is the first movement from Oneness into apparent duality. Once there is rhythm and movement, then there is time, and finally space. So all life and movement begins beyond time and ends in tangible space.

Mochin is beyond this world. The inner cosmic reason for creation is not openly revealed and in our own life most people are emotionally reactive. An objective of the Mitzvah of tefillin is to draw down Mochin, mind, meaning the Transcendent aspect of life and higher light, into the world at large, and into the 'small universe', which is us, so that our hearts and actions are aligned with the true purpose of creation (*Shar Ha'Kavanos*, Kerias Shema, p.138. See *Tikunei Zohar*. Hakdamah, 9a).

As a child reaches the age of thirteen, the mind has presumably developed sufficiently to begin to attempt to consider the sense of their life purpose, and thus, they can begin to put on tefillin and draw down higher Keser and Mochin into their life.

When each letter of Hashem's Name, which represents beyond time, is individually squared and then added together, the total equals 186. This is the same numerical equivalent as the Hebrew word for space, or place, *Makom*. Hashem — Yud/10, Hei/5, Vav/6, Hei/5. Ten times ten, five times five, six times six and five times five = 186. *Makom* — Mem/40, Kuf/100, Vav/6, Mem/40 =186.

The Maggid of Mezritch teaches that the word tefillin comes from the word *Tofel*, meaning connected and bound (see also, *Zohar III*, 10b). The essential idea of this concept of connecting and binding as it relates to the name of Hashem is to connect the *Yud* of Chochmah, wisdom and higher intelligence, with the final *Hei* of Malchus, the world of receptivity and action. In short, to connect Thought with Action.

Thus the word tefillin is spelled like *Tofel*, but with an additional Yud and Nun. The *Yud* represents Chochmah, and the *Nun* (which equals 50) represents the fullness of the final *Hei*. Hei equals 5, so when the final Hei, the ultimate receiver, is filled with all of the 10 Sefiros, the total is 50 (*Zohar III*, 63b).

By drawing down Mochin from the Four letters in Hashem's name, starting from the dot at the top of the *Yud* (the Keser, the beyond), down into our place — our *Makom*, our reality — into the world at large, the 'square' dimensional, limited universe, we are transforming the very fabric of this world, and most importantly, ourselves.

SPIRITUAL ATTRIBUTES OF THE STRAPS OF THE TEFILLIN

From the boxes and the scrolls contained within, flow the straps. First the straps encircle the crown of the head. One direction of strap surrounding the right side of the head, which represents the emotional attribute of *Chesed* or kindness, the other strap surrounding the left part of the head, representing the attribute of *Gevurah* or strength and restraint. Then tied in the back of the head is a knot, which has the shape of a *Dalet*, for the word *Da'as*.

The place of the knot is right below the skull where the head meets the neck (*Rambam*, see however, *Ohr Zaruah*, 876). This area of the head is connected with the Da'as part of the brain, the cerebellum, or 'little brain'. The attribute of Da'as is connected with both the front and the rear of the brain (Rashab, *Sefer Hamamorim, Ayin Ches*, p 146). Correspondingly, the *Luz* bone is right below the skull (*HaAruch*, Erech Luz. *Avodas Hakodesh*, 2, 40). So the place of the knot, in the shape of a Dalet, is situated right against the Luz Bone (*Sefer Likutim*, Shoftim, 4). It is with this small bone, which does not succumb to the ravages of worms or any other natural putrefaction, that we will experience resurrection (*Medrash*

Rabbah, Bereishis 28:3. *Bava Kama* 16b, *Tosefos*). The Luz bone is our link to immortality.

So the knot represents Da'as, and the straps represent Chesed and Gevurah. The root of these two straps is Chochmah, wisdom, circling the right hemisphere of the brain, and Binah, circling the left hemisphere of the brain. And they both flow from Keser (*Pardes Rimon*, Shar Hatzinoros).

Now, from that point of the knot, placed in the middle of the back of the head, flow the two straps, one to the right and one to the left. The knot therefore represents the reality of the middle column, namely, the sefira of Da'as, knowledge, and also connected with the middle column sefira of Tiferes, beauty, harmony and compassion.

The straps flow from this knot, i.e. from the middle column, one to the right and one to the left, representing the general flow of the emotional attributes of Chesed or kindness to the right side, and Gevurah or strength and restraint to the left. For this reason, the right strap hangs lower then the left, for we wish to draw down more right column Chesed then left column Gevurah.

In actuality, the right strap hanging down from the head is the outward expression of Chesed, which is also a right column attribute, the attribute of *Netzach*, or victory, ambition and perseverance. And the left strap hanging down from the head is the outward expression of Gevurah, which is also a left column attribute, the attribute of *Hod*, splendor, devotion and humility *(Derech Mitzvosecha*, Tefillin 2).

In truth, Chesed and Gevurah emanate from the same space, the transcendental knot interweaving both of these elements, rooted in the deepest place of Keser (also along the Middle Column), the blackness, the level beyond comprehension which is called "the light out of darkness".

It should be pointed out that although the actual boxes can be any color, according to Halacha, the custom is to paint them black *(Rosh*, Hilchos Tefillin 8. *Rambam*, Tefillin, 3:14). Beyond the aesthetic aspect of painting the boxes black, there is a spiritual significance, as the boxes represent Keser, the hidden Light.

So while both these spiritual/energetic flows (the straps) originate in Keser and the knot or middle column of Da'as and Tiferes, nevertheless, we seek to draw down Chesed into dominant revelation. We always want more Chesed than Gevurah. And even when we need to exhibit Gevurah, we should do so from a place of Chesed.

Da'as is the key to our emotions. Its development and alignment will determine the openness and flow of the proceeding attributes, either right or left, giving or restraining, openness or confinement, extroversion or introversion. The hanging straps represent the flow of consciousness downward, and though their source, leather, is the same as the white parchment — the Makif beyond letters and comprehension — they must be colored with the darkness of black dye, reflecting both a descent below the level of parchment, becoming more dense and black, as well as an origin above the parchment, as in the black of the Batim or boxes. Therefore they represent the highest level of Keser, the black, projected into the lowest and densest of vessels, Malchus.

Hanging lower on the right side, the right strap reaches until the point of the Bris, the place of the circumcision, which is the Sefira of Yesod, connected with Tiferes by way of the upper middle column, and with Malchus by way of the lower middle column (*Shalah*, *Chulin*, Torah Ohr 4, Tefillin). Creating a unity between all that is balanced Above and all that is balanced below.

This idea about the straps and their relationship with the Midos, the emotions and character attributes, and the color black needs more elucidation. The right strap around the head is Chesed and the left strap around the head is Gevurah. The strap hanging down to the right is the attribute of Netzach, and the strap hanging down to the left is the attribute of Hod. They are each hanging downwards until Yesod and Malchus, respectively. So all in all, the straps represent the Midos, and as such, the straps — coming from the 'head' — lay upon the heart (Tiferes), the seat of our emotions. The hand straps are wrapped around the arm, seven times, also corresponding to the seven Midos.

So we can see that the straps are connected with the Midos. On the other hand, however, the straps are painted black, which represents transcendence — something too intense to be revealed, the level of Keser, beyond Mochin, or mind — and they actually emanate from the Batim, the boxes, which are the Makifim. But are the Midos really above and below Mochin?

The answer is that the root of Midos is beyond Mochin. As the Zohar says, "*Zha B'Atika Achid V'Tali*", "the seven emotions are dependent on and one with Transcendence". Yet, it is the Mochin, the mind, that guides the emotions. Our emotions develop according to our intelligence. Younger children desire one set of things, and adults desire another. As our intelligence develops so do our emotions. But in truth, the raw emotion, the desire, is the same for a young child as an adult. It is just the focus of the desire that changes.

The Tzemach Tzedek offers a parable to explain this dynamic *(Derech Mitzvhasecha,* Tefillin, 2). The story is of a person who tells another person that in a certain place there is a treasure that is hidden, and because of this information the person gets excited to go seek the treasure. The first person did not create the emotion of excitement within the second person, he just directed him, and his emotions were aroused. The point of this parable is that the intellect is just directing our desires; showing us where to look, what we should pursue, what pleasures we should seek based on our understanding of the purpose of life. So the intellect guides us, but the emotions themselves are deeper than our intellect.

The objective of the tefillin, especially the head tefillin, is to draw down higher Keser and Mochin into our lives. Yet, before one can draw upon this transendenent level of Keser and Mochin he needs to ensure that his own vessels are fully equipped and prepared to absorb that which he is able to access. If he draws down Keser and Mochin and his vessels are unfit to receive, he will shatter the vessels. Higher, deeper intellect revealed to someone before they are emotionally equipped is meaningless and fruitless, and may even be damaging. Much like a person who understands intellectually that they should not engage in a certain pattern of beheviour, yet they are not quite ready emotionally for the ramifications of this understanding. Besides this premature understanding being ineffective, it can actually cause even more harm, for now this person will be living with an internal conflict and charged polar dichotomy. They will know something to be true in their mind, but still they are not acting accordingly. This can produce feelings of guilt or shame associated with not living up to one's perceived potential or intention. This is why, before one dons the head tefillin, he wraps the hand tefillin. So as to strengthen, align, and prepare the lower vessels to receive the light that is brought down from the higher vessels.

While the Bayis of the head tefillin represents Keser or *Zair Anpin* — the masculine, the *Partzuf* of Leah and

Moshiach Ben Dovid, and the Divine flow into the four forms of Mochin — the Bayis of the hand tefillin signifies Malchus, which corresponds to the *Partzuf* of Rochel and is connected with Moshiach Ben Yoseph. Malchus is the recipient of all the nine preceeding Divine emanations.

What exists in the head tefillin, written in four scrolls and placed in four separate compartments, is all written out in one scroll and included within one vessel in the hand tefillin *(Zohar ii, 43a)*. For the ultimate receiver is one, just as the ultimate Giver is One, and all the Sefiros are deposited into and manifested within the one vessel of Malchus.

From Malchus, we wrap the strap around our arm seven times — reflecting the seven emotional Sefiros — literally binding and linking our emotions and our actions in complete dedication, ready to receive the deepest levels of Mochin.

Whereas the head tefillin has four compartments, the hand tefillin has one, and thus represents the feminine aspect. The one hollow compartment reflects the womb, the origin of birth, and the straps that flow from the one box, and are wrapped around the arms reflect the umbilical cord.

Certainly there is Mochin as well at the level of the hand, reflected in the physical world, the world of action. However, it is the Mochin connected with our emotional state, emotional intelligence, as it were. For every level of reality contains the entire *Partzuf*, the complete internal structure of the ten Sefiros, including Mochin (intellect), Middos (emotions) and Ma'asim (actions).

And so, in the hand tefillin we find the entire Partzuf or all ten sefiros. First we place the Bayis around our upper arm and then wrap the straps around the biceps another two times. Three straps in total, corresponding to the three basic levels of intellect — Chochmah/Wisdom, Binah/cognition, and Da'as/knowledge. Then we wrap the strap seven times around the forearm aligned with the seven emotional attributes, the Midos, concluding with wrapping the strap around the middle finger and palm of our hand reflecting the world of action.

Of course, just as there is Mochin in Middos, the hand tefillin, there are Middos in Mochin, the head tefillin. The head tefillin, which is Mochin, contains the three pronged Shin, representing the three basic forms of intelligence, as well as the four compartments and the four pronged Shin, corresponding to the three forms of intelligence plus the power of imagination. Yet, as the Zohar teaches *(iii, p.288a)*, in total there are seven prongs to the Shins, and they correspond to the *"seven maids suitable to be given to her from the Kings home"*, which simply means the seven emotional Sefiros, the Midos. So the head also embodies the seven emotional and lower Sefiros.

Once this order is in place, having aligned our emotions and actions, secured them, and made prepared ourselves to receive a taste of the "light that comes out of darkness", we put on the head tefillin and allow for the new Mochin to enter. Having bound our reality as is in total dedication — represented by the hand tefillin —we can put on the tefillin of the head and draw down a much deeper, more profound measure of Mochin — a Mochin from the future world of perfect unity, ensuring a perfect alignment between our deepest levels of body, heart, mind, and soul.

CHAPTER V:

THE AGE OF BAR MITZVAH & MENTAL MATURITY

CHAPTER V:
THE AGE OF BAR MITZVAH &
MENTAL MATURITY

The age of thirteen is the age of maturity, when a boy begins to become a man. This existential shift is also accompanied by actual physical changes in the body as the body is transitioning from that of a child into an adult *(Nidah,* 46a*)*. This period is a major life cycle event and rite of passage. From this day forward, the young boy has embarked on the journey of becoming a man, a person with responsibility. From now on, the young boy has begun to become conscious of developing the ability to recognize right from wrong, what is good and what is bad, as well as a healthy sense of the consequences of ones actions.

The term *Bar Mitzvah* literally means the son of a Mitzvah. From this point on, the young man becomes responsible for performing and upholding the Mitzvos of the Torah.

Thirteen, for boys, is the age of Mitzvah *(Avos,* 5:21*)*. Mitzvah simply means commandment, but on a deeper level Mitzvah comes from the word meaning connection *(Degel Machanah Ephraim.* Korach. *Likutei Torah,* Bechukosai, 45c). From this point forward, the boy becomes more connected to the Torah and assumes more responsibility for the Mitzvos and to the development of his Jewish, spiritual identity, to the Jewish people as a community, and by extension to the entire world.

Our reality is primarily an emotionally based reality and the way most people live life is through unconscious, reactive, emotional responses to external circumstances and stimulus. Instinct and emotional feelings, for better — as in love or connection — or worse — as in hate and fear — predominate most people's decisions about life. It is often rare to find clarity of thought, expansive thinking and openness of mind. This is because the Keser — resolute purpose — and the mature deliberation of Mochin are above the world so to speak, they are not a natural given. We need to mature and develop in order to receive them. Our purpose — and the means to attain it — does not always seem so apparent and needs to be revealed to us.

When a child reaches the age of thirteen, their minds have developed sufficiently to rationalize decisions, to make choices, to exhibit some control over themselves — if they truly desire to. And they can therefore begin to put on tefillin with the intention to draw down a sense of their personal and spiritual purpose, as well as a revelation of a deeper sense of Mochin into their reality, filtered down through their Midos, until the truth of this higher revealed reality infuses their entire way of being and acting. For once there is a proper and prepared vessel, i.e. the maturity of heart and mind, one can then attempt to draw down *Gadlus Ha'mochin* or expansive mind.

Thirteen is the age of the beginning of mental maturity. Now, although, the age thirteen as a time where a child begins to mature and take on responsibility for Mitzvos is *Halacha l'Moshe m'-Sinai*, traditions given by Moshe at Sinai. *(Teshuvas Ha'Rosh,* 16;1. *Mishnah Berurah,* 55;40). Meaning, that the Torah establishes the directive that at thirteen— for a boy, — and twelve for a girl — the child becomes a young adult, and can be responsible for themselves as independent people.

We do find an allusion to this idea of maturing at thirteen in the Torah regarding the sons of Yaakov. When the two brothers, Shimon and Levi, took it upon themselves to avenge the violation of their sister, they were called 'Men' *(Bereishis,* 34:25*).* They had a sense of justice and righteousness, and took action. It is taught that Levi, the younger of the two, turned thirteen on that day (The Lubavitcher Rebbe, *Reshima's).*

One of the first steps of maturity is becoming more sensitive to the needs and interests of others, besides oneself.

In the case of Shimon and Levi, this was demonstrated in their sensing the distress of their sister. The second step is to do something about it, taking personal responsibility for justice and righteousness. It is not sufficient to know right from wrong, but rather, one must stand up for what is right and make sure that there is no perpetuation of what is wrong.

Overall, at the age of thirteen, a boy begins to have more mindful awareness and, by extension, the ability to be more responsible.

EXPANSIVE MIND
& CONSTRICTED MIND

Being that the age of thirteen is the beginning of maturity, it is also the age that tefillin — along with the recitation of their accompanying blessings — begin to be worn, starting from the day of the boy's Bar Mitzvah.

As previously explored in great detail, through the Mitzvah of tefillin we draw down flashes and flows of novel and elevated Mochin, intelligence, and especially *Gadlus Ha'-Mochin*, big or expansive mind, which is connected with mental maturity.

Overall, children experience *Katnus Ha'Mochin*, small, constricted or immature mind. They may be smart and intelligent, but overall, children lack a certain sense of maturity and the ability to perceive the big picture. The basic difference between these two states, between Gadlus and Katnus, is the difference between a mature adult and an immature child (*Maamorei Admur Hazoken*. Inyonim, p. 201). The bigger or more expanded the mind is, the more inclusive it becomes, and the more it encompasses. An adult with a mature mind is capable of contemplating simultaneous opposites and paradox, without breaking down into false conflict and duality. They can understand that the losing of one thing often means the gaining of something greater, perhaps in the future.

Give a child a dollar to buy candy and then tell them that if they give you back the dollar today, you will give them two dollars tomorrow, and see what happens. For the child, what is now is now. When a favorite toy is taken away from a child, or is broken, the child loses himself completely and it is hard to comfort them. You cannot explain to them that you will by them another, better toy tomorrow. They cannot sustain paradox, simultaneous opposites, or tension. Their minds are one dimensional, as it were.

A child has Mochin, mind. He can figure things out, he knows how to open the box to his toys and maybe even build them. But his Mochin is *Katnus*, small, immature, constricted.

Children cannot and should not put on tefillin.

The idea of tefillin is to draw down *Mochin D'gadlus*, big picture mind into our lives. When a child reaches a mature age, he can and should put on tefillin.

STAGES OF DEVELOPMENT

In the general development of the human being there are three main stages:

1.   *Ibbur* — pregnancy
2.   *Yenikah* — nursing
3.   *Mochin* — mind, consciousness

But when seen in more specific detail, one can actually perceive five stages:

1.   *Zeri'ah* — Sowing of the seed
2.   *Ibbur* — Pregnancy
3.   *Leidah* — Birthing
4.   *Yenikah* — Nursing
5.   *Mochin* —mind, consciousness.

These two separate but complementary models are the three/five stages of maturation, from conception all the way to full independence and self-awareness. In the process of development — whether physical, psychological, or spiritual — the preceeding stage is always Katnus in comparison to the proceeding stage, which is Gadlus. And the stage that is Gadlus in comparison to the preceeding stage is viewed as Katnus in relation to the next proceeding stage. This developmental process is illustrative of a movement from mere extension and dependence towards independence and uniqueness.

We will explore both of these models (the three and the five stage models of development) in greater depth throughout the following pages. As mentioned previously, they are each meant to be seen as complete in and of themselves, as well as meant to be overlayed and viewed in relation to each other. It is a standard approach of Kabbalah specifically, and Torah in general, to provide numerous lenses and perspectives through which to view a single idea or phenomenon. This associative technique is not meant to confuse the reader, but rather to give the honest seeker as many tools as possible with which to plumb the depths of their existence and experience of the world.

We will begin by taking a deeper look at the five-stage model of development.

Here are the five main stages in the process of becoming in greater detail:

1) *Zeri'ah*
   Sowing of the seed, the moment of conception. This is the first stage towards birth and individuality. In the stage of Zeri'ah there is no individual, the individual is completely hidden and undetectable.

2) *Ibbur*

The second stage is impregnation, much like a fetus within the womb of the mother. Here the embryo has taken on form and its existence can now be detected. Yet, there is no independence and the child is one with his mother, literally an extension of the mother. Such as it says in the Gemara, the 'fetus is like the limb of the mother' *(Chulin,* 58a*)*.

3) *Leidah*

The third stage is birthing. Now the infant is fully formed, and all can see that it exists as an independent entity, no longer attached, literally speaking, to the mother.

4) *Yenikah*

The fourth stage is nursing, where a child is outside the womb, starting to move about, yet, completely dependent on the mother for its survival.

5) *Mochin*

The fifth stage is Mochin or mind and maturity, where the child becomes independent, rational, and understanding of self and others.

These five general stages of early human development correspond to the five times the word *Ohr*, Light, appears in the Torah during the creation story. Ohr is the first 'thing' to be created, and thus the model of creation.

WRAPPED IN MAJESTY: TEFILLIN

1) *"Let there be light"* (*Bereishis*, 1:3).
This is Zeriah, the "sowing of the seed",
expressing the potential for desired conception.

2) *"And there was light"* *(ad loc.* 1:3*).*
This is Ibbur, the time of "impregnation".
The light exists, but is still hidden, gestating.

3) *"G-d saw that the light was good"* *(ad loc.* 1:4*).*
This is Leidah, the "birthing" stage.
There is now an ability to perceive and experience the
light, as it is birthed into existence.

4) *"G-d separated the light from darkness"* *(ad loc.* 1:4*).*
This is Yenikah, the "nursing" stage.
This process is characterized by the completion of the
dependent stage, which occurs towards the end of the
nursing stage, when the child is 'separated' from its
mother and weaned off of the mother's milk.

5) *"G-d called the light Day"* *(ad loc.* 1:5*).*
This is Mochin, the independent stage wherein the
child begins to develop a 'mind' of their own.
The initial light now becomes a potential source of
light, as now the child may too become a parent.

We will now return to the three-stage model of development. Corresponding to the three main stages of development outlined above (Ibbur, Yenikah, Mochin), there are

also three basic levels of soul and spiritual complexity through which the child evolves and enters into throughout their life.

The three basic levels of soul are *Nefesh*, *Ruach*, and *Neshama*.

1. *Nefesh* is connected with *Ibbur*
2. *Ruach* is connected with *Yenikah*
3. *Neshamah* is connected with *Mochin*

Nefesh is the soul level we are born with. In fact, our Nefesh enters us at our conception, even while in a state of Ibbur *(Medrash Talpiyos)*. From the moment of conception we already have a semblance of an instinct of survival, it is our animating, sustaining, and physical growth aspect of soul. This primal level is one that we have in common with all living creatures.

Nefesh is associated with our blood, with our liver, and with our digestive system. Nefesh is our subtle bio-energy, also known as the animating element, connected to our instincts and sensory experiences. Our instinct to survive is an expression of Nefesh.

Ruach is the level of soul that enters us at a young age, beginning with our Yenikah state. Our Ruach is more subtle than the almost tangible Nefesh, which is perceived through physicality and raw life. Emotions, desires (which require communication for their fulfillment), and creative expressions are part of our Ruach consciousness. Ruach, which is also translated as 'wind', is thus connected with speech, an articulate wind or breath.

Ruach is our emotional reality, our ability and willingness to express our inner experience. This can manifest in joy, smiles, and laughter, or in tears, screams, and tantrums. Children have lots of ruach.

The third level of soul is *Neshamah*. Neshamah is our conscious and rational selves.

Neshamah is the level of soul that enters us at maturity. Beginning, for a boy, at the age of thirteen and then becoming more integrated at the age of twenty. At this age the boy is now more of a man. He is both capable and experienced in abstract reasoning and more acute in financial matters. Finally, the Neshamah is more fully absorbed and internalized at the age of forty. Thus, the word Neshamah is comprised of the words, *Mem*, forty, and *Shanah*, years *(Nitzutuzei Zohar* 1, p. 191a).

Neshamah is generally known as the *Yetzer Ha'tov,* the good inclination, as will be explored shortly.

Mochin, or intellectual maturity, as well as the physical development of the brain, allows for the Neshamah to enter, or begin entering, at the age of thirteen.

THREE STAGES OF DEVELOPMENT AND THEIR CORRESPONDING BODY POSITIONS

These three developmental states and levels of soul — Ibbur/Nefesh, Yenikah/Ruach, and Mochin/Neshamah — also correspond to three bodily positions:

1) Lying Down
2) Sitting
3) Standing

Lying down is Ibbur. This represents a state of zero independence, where the child is not even able to sit up on its own. Left to its own devices, a young infant can only lie down. While in the position of lying down, the head, i.e. the mind, and the rest of the body, even the feet, are on the same horizontal level, which represents that there is no dominance or chain of command of mind over instinct. In this alignment, all cognitive capacities are considered the same. This is the consciousness of Nefesh or pure instinct.

Next step is the movement from lying down to sitting up. This is a major development for a child, which requires a modicum of strength, balance, and self-control. Here the child is gaining more independence. They are big enough to sit up by themselves. This is the state of Yenikah. When the body is in a sitting position, the most prominent and revealed part of the body is the torso, the seat of the heart and

metaphorical home of our emotions. This is the consciousness of Ruach — emotional reality.

The final step is to stand up erect and full upright. This is
a unique position of the human being. A standing position
suggests that there is a flow from top to bottom. There is a
movement from the mind, to the heart, to the instincts and
actions. The mind dictates. This is advanced Mochin. This
is the consciousness of Neshamah.

THE SPIRITUAL SIGNIFICANCE OF
THE THREE BODY POSITIONS

Lying down is Katnus in comparison to sitting up, whereas
sitting is Katnus in comparison to standing.

Everyday, even as an adult, upon awakening we move
through these three stages. During the night we lay down,
then as we wake up, we first sit up, and than we stand. This
daily cycle is a microcosm of the process of our birth and
eventual maturation. First we lay down, than we sit up, and
then we learn to stand fully erect on our own two feet.

Sleeping is Katnus in comparison to sitting and waking
up, and certainly compared to being awake and standing.

When a human being lies down to sleep they lay down
completely, and some even curl up on their side, resembling
the position of a fetus in the womb. This represents the first

stage of life, *Ibbur*, pregnancy. Sleep is a resting period, a time out, a much needed, nurturing, and therapeutic condition — so as to be more focused, alert and productive upon awakening.

In fact, everything in life — from animals to plants and even the oceans, for example — experiences these two movements, moving from Katnus to Gadlus *(Imrei Pinchas)*. For example in Katnus, a tree is still contained within its seed or is losing its leaves; in Gadlus that same tree is flowering or giving forth fruit. In Katnus, the ocean is in low tide or is just quiet and tranquil; in Gadlus, it is in high tide or is swelling and turbulent.

In all cases, the Katnus of a thing is the complete inverse image of its Gadlus state. And so, in the case of human beings, whose Gadlus state is represented by standing up and walking about, their Katnus state of sleep is a total reclining to the point of lying down, sometimes even curling up, resembling the fetal position. As the Gadlus of the human being is the greatest of all creatures, so is their Katnus, as there is no other creature as underdeveloped physically at birth as the human. This is why human babies experience what is referred to as the 'fourth trimester' outside the womb.

Nefesh — Ibbur — Lying Down
Ruach — Yenikah — Sitting up
Neshamah — Mochin — Standing and Walking About

We put on tefillin when we are in a condition of standing up, during the day. The Torah refers to the day as a time when people stand *(Devarim, 6:7)*. When we are awake and standing, we are now in the position to draw down *Shefa*, Divine Influx, from a more expansive level of Mochin through the act of putting on the tefillin.

When we are laying down our head and our backside are on an even plane, the head is not elevated above the rest of the body. This is also symbolic of an animal on all fours, where for the most part the head, the heart, and the backside are all evenly aligned.

When we are sitting up, and certainly when we stand erect, the head is above the heart, and the heart above the backside.

Having the head above the heart and sitting on top of the body is symbolic of Mochin, mind, and specifically *Mochin D'gadlus*, or expansive mind. Whereas the position of the body that places the head equal to the heart and body, as in an adult laying down or a child before learning how to sit up, is symbolic of *Mochin D'katnus*, small or constricted mind.

Children, and sadly, some adults who act like children, have overwhelming Katnus. This is when their body, hearts, and mind are all on the same level, as in the position of lying down. Simply put, when life feels unfair, miserable, or hopeless, they begin crying hysterically or throwing a tantrum because their bodies have to relieve this tension, and crying is a release. Or when someone shames them, they feel completely inadequate due to the fact that their self-image is totally dependent on external acceptance or the opposite. Essentially, an immature person is in such a state of development that the mind is on the same level of their emotions and body. There is no 'mind' control, as in putting things into the proper context and perspective. This results in an inability to tolerate life's inevitable paradoxes or anomalies.

A standing up or erect individual, a real adult, is one who has Mochin, so that they can put events into context. Just because you really need to relieve yourself of accumulated tension or stress does not mean that your life is over. From this perspective, one is able to react to circumstances in a far less dramatic and impulsive manner.

Even within the state of 'mature mind' there are levels beyond levels. Every Gadlus is considered Katnus in comparison to a higher Gadlus. You can never stop growing, developing, expanding, and moving from level to level, always embracing more of reality. In fact, this is the essence of our spiritual work, to perceive the inner/concealed light within every idea and experience, to continuously strive to reach new heights of perception and perfection, and to never give up.

Deeper still, Gadlus does not only imply achieving a state

of *Mochin*, or mind, awareness, or conscious control of one's emotions and instincts, but also implies a certain maturity in one's capacity to accept the existence of paradox and to entertain seemingly conflicting ideas simultaneously. This includes giving weight and importance to the needs of the body, being sensitive to the stirrings of the heart, and yet at the same time, maintaining a clear and subtle state of mind, all at once.

Even deeper, an adult who has arrived at a certain semblance of Mochin is generally guided by a sound rationale, and yet they can still exist in a devastating or crippling level of Katnus; for instance, a Katnus of the ego, in the form of a perpetual self–serving approach to life that seeks only instant gratification.

We all have various inner voices. Traditionally these are called the *Yetzer Ha'ra*, the negative inclination, or selfish impulse, and the *Yetzer Ha'tov*, the good inclination or selfless impulse *(Berachos, 61a)*. Our yetzer ha-ra is very wily, conniving, and manipulative. *"It first appears to us as a modest traveler with a humble opinion. Then (if not recognized for what it is) it evolves into a welcomed guest, and finally (if we're not careful) becomes the master of the house"* *(Sukkah, 52a)*. Yet, at the same time, the yetzer ha-ra is also called a fool *(Koheles, 4:13, Rashi)*. It does indeed have mind, but it is a foolish mind.

The main reason for its foolishness is that the yetzer ha'ra seeks only what is rewarding in the moment. In a state of spiritual alienation, a human being's thinking is limited and confined, only thinking in the immediate short term, with no regard for the future (*Akeidas Yitzchak*. Parshas Naso, Shar 73.) It is foolish because its perception is of separation, in time, as in the present being separate from the past or future, and deeper still, a total sense of separation within and from everything. And when separation is the only mode of consciousness available, one is fundamentally in conflict with others and even within oneself.

The yetzer ha-ra is the force that instructs a person to seek that which seems rewarding in the moment, with total disregard for past commitments or future repercussions. It is the consciousness that observes reality only through the prism of a two-dimensional lens and, therefore, it pursues the image, the surface, the immediate and the materialistic.

This is the small, and essentially limiting, 'i'.

Gadlus is when we are not guided by the small i of immediate gratification. When we can behold the big picture — past, present and future interwoven as one experiential tapestry of being — the transcendence-centered yetzer ha-tov beholds reality as it truly is. It sees that the diversity of the physical universe is interconnected and permeated by *Achdus*, the unity of the Creator and of all Creation. In this mode of consciousness, all concealment and separation appears only on the surface and is transparent to an underlying awareness of the absolute unity both above and within all of Creation.

Through the Mitzvah of tefillin we have the ability to draw down Mochin D'gadlus into our lives. And as we wrap tefillin every day, we have the ability to constantly access ever deepening and expanding levels of Gadlus. And what is considered Gadlus today is, compared with the abilities and perceptions we may reach tomorrow, small and constricted. Every single day, in fact, every moment, if we are able to remain aware and open to our soul's yearning and desire for spirituality and unity, even the immediate past looks small in comparison to the eternal present. We need to be continually moving forward, lest we slip backwards. If we are not moving up, we are moving down. There is no such thing as standing still; the universe is constantly in motion. Every step we take, whether deeper or higher, shows us that the previous rung was small and limited compared to the present view.

BAR MITZVAH AS A RITE OF PASSAGE FOR BOTH FATHER & SON

According to the Zohar, On the day of a boy's Bar Mitzvah, we need to make a festive meal, as on the day of ones wedding (*Zohar Chadash*, Bereishis, 10*)*. It is a joyous time, and one that should be celebrated (*Magen Avraham*, Orach Chaim, 225:4). But like all transitions in life, even the joyous ones, there is always a measure of gentle sadness.

The age of Bar Mitzvah is a transitional stage, and as is the case with every transition, there is a mix of the joy of moving on, as well as the bittersweet melancholy of leaving what was, behind. The child is now officially growing up and becoming a man. He is no longer in the stage of *Yenikah*, suckling, both feeding off of and clinging to the parents, almost attached to their hip, as it were. Now begins the awkward stage of adolescence. The young boy will go off to Yeshiva and may even board and live away from home. Eventually, the young boy will become a fully-grown man and move away from his parental home and establish his own household. So while there is great joy, having merited to witness and participate in the growth of this young boy, there is also a sense of sadness on the part of the parents.

There is an inner tension that parents feel when their children begin maturing. On the one hand, the sense of pride and perhaps relief to have brought them to this place. And yet, on the other hand, an underlining sense of anxiety, knowing that the nurturing period of their child's life, which began at birth, is now coming to a close. This transitional stage of the parents sets in motion an awareness of their own mortality and ageing.

When a boy reaches the age of thirteen, growing up and becoming Bar Mitzvah, he is becoming essentially "old enough to protect" and to be responsible. It is now time, our sages tell us, "for the *father* to *buy* him tefillin" (*Sukkah*, 42a).

And so, besides the Bar Mitzvah celebration, which is written about in the Zohar and is considered a *Seudas Mitzvah*, a meal of a Mitzvah *(Yam Shel Shlomo)*, as the boy is becoming a man, it is the father who needs to buy him the tefillin. The actual purchasing of the tefillin by the father marks, acknowledges, and in essence, eases this transition.

A child who is Bar Mitzvah is old enough to protect and respect the sanctity of the Torah and its Mitzvos, including his tefillin, and thus his father buys him a pair. As it is written, "When the child turns thirteen, and not before, his father buys him a pair of tefillin" *(Itur.* See: *Beis Yoseph*, O'C, 37). There is a strong emphasis on the father buying the tefillin for his son (*Tosefos, Erchin* 2b).

The father's act of purchasing and passing on the tefillin to his son at the time of Bar Mitzvah is the passing of the torch of Torah, of tradition, of heritage, of history, of eternity, and indeed of our immortality. It is a testament, an Os, of our sense of and connection to eternity in the face of the temporary. This rite of passage — buying, giving, and helping the Bar Mitzvah put on the tefillin for the very first time — is the Torah's way of lifting us all — as individuals, as a family, and as a community — to the highest heights of eternity, immortality and transcendence.

THE PRACTICALITIES
OF TEFILLIN

USEFUL INFORMATION

UPKEEP OF THE TEFILLIN

1. STORING TEFILLIN

When not in use, tefillin should be placed in their properly fitting cases, and then placed within a special dedicated bag. We need to 'protect' our Tefillin.

Tefillin are called an *Os*, a 'sign', similar to *Shabbos*. Just as Shabbos needs to be 'remembered' and 'protected', the same is true with tefillin. We need to remember the tefillin, by putting them on, and 'protect' them by placing them in a secure and protected place.

Tefillin are dedicated for holy purposes, and should be treated with particular honor. Thus it is inappropriate to bring tefillin into a bathroom. In a public place (such as an airport, with no safe place to guard the tefillin bag), in which one is afraid that if left alone the tefillin will be stolen or tampered with, one may enter a modern restroom facility, by placing the tefillin bag within another bag or covering it with their jacket, coat, or any other garment so that the tefillin bag itself is covered.

Tefillin are made of leather and must retain their black color. So they should not be exposed to climatic extremes, whether of heat, cold, or moisture.

2. CHECKING TEFILLIN

It is best to have one's tefillin checked periodically, at least once every four years, and if possible once a year. Traditionally, this is done during the month of Elul preceding the High Holidays.

If one begins to notice any rounding on the corners of the boxes of the tefillin, or paint chipping (particularly on the straps), have them checked immediately.

The laws of tefillin are detailed and complex, so it is imperative that they be checked by a qualified professional *Sofer*, 'scribe', to ensure that they are kosher for use.

BASIC LAWS OF TEFILLIN

1) The obligation to put on tefillin begins at *Bar mitzvah*, at the age of thirteen. Customarily, one begins to wear tefillin two months before the Bar Mitzvah (initially without the blessing).

2) Tefillin are put on every weekday, preferably in the morning, ideally during the morning prayers. However, if for some reason one did not put on tefillin in the morning, one may put them on with their accompanying blessing until sunset.

3) On Shabbos and *Yom Tov*, the 'Festivals', including (according to most customs) the intermediate days of *Sukkos* and of *Pesach*, tefillin are *not* worn.

4) On *Chanukah* and *Purim*, tefillin *are* worn.

5) On *Tisha B'av*, the 'ninth day of the month of Av', the day we mourn the destruction of the Holy Temple, tefillin

are not worn in the morning. Instead, one should put on his tefillin for the afternoon *Minchah* prayer service.

6) When a *Tallis*, 'prayer shawl', is worn during prayers, one should first wrap himself in the tallis and then put on the tefillin. At the conclusion of the prayers, the order is reverse. First, remove the tefillin and then take off the tallis.

7) One should make sure the body is physically clean when wearing tefillin, and that there is no need for the restroom.

8) If while wearing the tefillin one feels the need to relieve oneself, remove the tefillin and go to the restroom. Then put them on again with the preceding blessing. If for any other reason one needed to take off the tefillin, when putting them on again do so without the preceding blessing, so long as 2-3 hours have not elapsed since taking them off.

9) When wearing tefillin, one should not sit down to a meal. Though it is technically permissible to have a quick drink or light snack while wearing tefillin, in our times — in which tefillin are only worn for a short period each day — it is best not to eat or drink, unless it's absolutely necessary.

10) When wearing tefillin, one should try to be continuously mindful of them, directing ones thoughts to their prayers or to Torah study.

FREQUENTLY
ASKED QUESTIONS

Q) On which hand should a left-handed person place the hand tefillin?

A) Just as a right-handed person puts the tefillin on his "weaker" arm (the left), a left-handed person should put them on his "weaker" hand, (i.e. the right hand).

Q) If one is ambidextrous, on which hand should he place the tefillin?

A) Because each case is subtly unique, in such situations it is best to ask the local Rabbi. In the event that a competent authority is not immediately available to answer, however, the general rule is that the "stronger" hand with regards to putting on tefillin is the hand with which one writes. So if an ambidextrous person writes with his right hand he should put the tefillin on his left hand, and visa versa.

Q) What if the "weaker" arm (the one on which one would normally wrap tefillin) is covered in a cast, an Ace bandage, or the like? Where should the tefillin be worn?

A) Though generally tefillin are to be worn on the bare arm and head without any interventions, in this instance one may tie the box of the tefillin on the upper arm as usual, and then continue wrapping the straps around the cast or bandage.

Q) What if someone is missing completely his weak tefillin arm, can he just put on the head tefillin?

A) Yes, absolutely. He may just don the head tefillin. Before placing them on the head, he should recite two blessings — the usual blessing, *L'haniach Tefillin*, "to place tefillin", and the blessing, *Al Mitzvas Tefillin*, "on the Mitzvah of tefillin". This same law would apply, if for some reason one only has the head tefillin and does not have with him the hand tefillin.

Q) If, because of injury, one cannot put on the head tefillin, should the hand tefillin be put on anyway?

A) Yes, they are two separate Mitzvos, and even when one cannot put on both, he should put on the one he can.

Q) What happens if one put on the tefillin and then remembers that he forgot to make a blessing over them, can he say the blessing now?

A) Yes, as long as the tefillin are still on, one may recite the blessing.

Q) Hand tefillin are meant to be put on before the head tefillin. What happens if by mistake one took out the head tefillin from the tefillin bag first? Should one just continue and put the head tefillin on first?

A) The head tefillin should be put aside. Take the hand tefillin from the bag and put them on. Then continue with the head tefillin.

Q) What should one do if their tefillin accidentally fell to the floor?

A) If the tefillin were not covered in their cases, first make sure the edges were not damaged. In earlier generations, many people would fast as an atonement for allowing the tefillin to fall to the floor. Today, however, the custom is to redeem the fast with extra *Tzedakah* or 'charity'. One should offer the extra charity even if the tefillin fell when they were in their case.

For Further Reading on Tefillin, and how-to information for wrapping Tefillin, please see Rav Pinson's guide to donning Tefillin. 'A How-To Guide'
Available as a digital booklet on www.IYYUN.com

http://iyyun.com/booklets/tefillin-a-how-to-guide

QUOTES ABOUT TEFILLIN

TEACHINGS FROM THE GEMARAH, MEDRASH, AND CLASSIC TORAH SOURCES ON TEFILLIN

Tefillin are the strength of Israel *(Berachos, 6a)*.

Tefillin are the glory of Israel *(Sukkah, 25a)*.

Tefillin are called a gem *(Tosefos, Menachos, 34b)*.

And all the peoples of the world shall see that the name of G-d is called upon you, and they shall fear You. This, says R. Eliezer the Great, refers to the Tefillin of the head *(Berachos, 6a)*.

The root of dominance and oppression of other nations over the children of Israel is the laxity of Tefillin *(Adir Bamarom)*.

When asked in what merit was he worthy to live a long life, Rav Ada replied "I have always worn Tefillin" *(Ta'anis, 20b)*.

Once the celebrated sage Abaya was sitting at the seat of his teacher Rava who observed that he seemed very merry. He said: Is it not written, "And rejoice with trembling?" He replied: "I am putting on Tefillin" *(Berachos, 30b)*.

The Mitzvah of Tefillin is a Segulah, 'omen', for having boys *(Ben Yehoyadah, Eruvin, 96a)*.

Once someone had a dream in which his Tefillin were found to not be Kosher and was told to buy new Tefillin. The Arizal interpreted his dream that his wife was pregnant with a boy, but she will miscarry, and then she will become pregnant again with a healthy boy *(Shar Ruach Ha'kodesh)*.

"We deeply desire to toil in Torah day and night, we simply do not have the time", say the people of Israel. G-d responds, "Keep the Mitzvah of Tefillin and I will consider it as if you have studied Torah all day and night" *(Medrash Tehilim, 1)*.

Torah in its entirety is compared to Tefillin *(Makkos, 11a)*.

Whatever Hashem commands, He does Himself. G-d puts on Tefillin. And what is written in Hashem's Tefillin? "Who is like you, people of Israel, a nation one/unique on earth" *(Berachos, 6a)*.

Hashem puts on Tefillin. Just as our putting on Tefillin demonstrates our continuous desire to cleave to and come closer to G-d, the image of G-d putting on Tefillin indicates Hashem's deep desire to be one with us. This is similar to, "I am to my beloved and my beloved is to me" *(Maharsha, Berachos, 6a)*.

The deepest form of putting on Tefillin is the putting on of Tefillin by Hashem. There are various levels of putting on Tefillin. One level is 'physical', where the putting on of Tefillin wrestles with negativity, and tames our and cosmic negative reality. A higher level is where the putting on of Tefillin serves to draw down more Mochin, 'mind', awareness, presence, deeper/higher understanding, both for oneself and others. A higher level is where the purpose of the Tefillin is not for oneself, no matter how lofty a purpose, but simply to create "pleasure on High"; it is utterly selfless. Here one is no longer putting on the Tefillin, but rather, in a way, it is as if Hashem is putting on the Tefillin through him *(Likutei Halachos, Shluchim, 5)*.

Tefillin protect us. It once happened that the Roman government proclaimed a decree against Israel, that anyone putting on Tefillin will have his brains pierced — i.e. the place where the Head Tefillin is placed *(Rashi)*. Elisha put on his Tefillin and went outside to the marketplace. A Roman official spotted him, and Elisha ran away. The official chased after him. When Elisha saw that he was coming close to him, he removed the Tefillin from his head and held them in his

hand. The officer demanded, 'What is that in your hand?' Elisha replied, 'The wings of a dove.' Then he opened up his
hand, and inside were the wings of a dove. Since the people
of Israel are symbolically similar to a dove, just as the wings
of a dove protect the bird, the same is true with the Mitzvos,
i.e. they protect and elevate us *(Shabbos, 49a).*

Once a person puts on Tefillin the status of his physical body
is forever changed *(See: Rosh Hashanah, 17a).*

The moment a person wraps himself in Tefillin and sancti-
fies himself in them, he becomes a 'complete person' and
his is called one *(Zohar III, p. 81a).*

Tefillin are strapped to the body as a precious jewel is held
near to oneself *(Rashba, Berachos, 6a).*

Moshe was shown the knot of Hashem's Tefillin *(Menachos,
35b).* This means that Moshe was shown a visual image of
the procedure and method of how to put on Tefillin, with all
the intricate details *(R. Hai Goan).*

One who has committed negative acts which should, by the
spiritual laws of cause and effect, result in a negative consequence, the Mitzvah of Tefillin can protect him and not
allow persecution to attach itself to him *(Zohar, Tikunim).*

One who wears Tefillin is granted a long life *(Menachos, 44a),*
as it is written, "Hashem being upon them, they will
live" *(Yeshayahu, 38:16).* Which means, one who bears upon
himself the name of G-d will live.

Long life is granted to one who wears Tefillin. According to
the Arizal, this is because the four compartments of the
Head Tefillin correspond to the Four letters in the Name
Ehe'yeh, 'I will be': Aleph/1, Hei/5, Yud/10, Hei/5 = 21. And
the Four portions placed in those four compartments corre-

spond to the Four letters in the Name of Hashem: Yud/10, Hei/5, Vav/6, Hei/5 = 26. In addition, there are 21 names of Hashem in these four portions, also corresponding to the name Ehe'yeh. So, 21+26+21 = 68, same as the word Chaim, 'Life': Ches/8, Yud/10, Yud/10, Mem/40 = 68 *(Shar Ha'kavanos, Inyan Tefillin, 2)*.

Long life, (also) means a full life; i.e. the days themselves are long and fulfilled. Nothing is mere routine, monotone, or stale. This means that one should strive to sense every moment as a new beginning, every moment as a fresh moment, and a chance to begin anew *(Likutei Halachos, Tefillin, 5:45)*.

When our forefather Yaakov was wrestling with the angelic spirit of Eisav, and the angel became aware of Yaakov's Tefillin he was frightened and backed off *(Meam Loez, Ekev)*.

One who puts on Tefillin, wears Tzitzis, reads the Shema, and prays daily is guaranteed a portion in the World to Come, lives a long life, is cleansed of all negativity, and will be protected from all purging in the afterlife *(Tur, Orach Chaim, 37)*.

All destructive forces disperse and lack the strength to come near the person who is crowned with Tefillin *(Reishis Chachmah)*.

One who puts on (head) Tefillin pushes aside all negative forces and sublimates all concealments *(Ben Ish Chai, Ben Yehoyadah, Berachos, 6a)*.

Tefillin, similar to the Torah itself, is the sword that protects us from all harm. Being that the Torah is divided into the written and the oral, so too there is the head Tefillin, corresponding to the written dimensions of Torah, and the hand Tefillin, analogous to the oral aspect of Torah *(Ha'emek Davar, Bo)*.

One who leaves home wrapped in a Tallis with Tefillin upon his head and on his arm, the divine presence rests upon his head and two angels come along to accompany him, one to his right and one on the left *(Zohar iii, Zohar Chodash, Teruma)*.

One who is careful of putting on Tefillin each day, it is as if he has fulfilled the entire six hundred and thirteen Mitzvos *(Reishis Chachmah)*.

A person who walks about holding something precious in their hands is constantly being watchful and afraid of being robbed. However, one who wears Tefillin has nothing to be apprehensive or scared about, as the seal of The King is upon you *(Akeidas Yitzchak, 90)*.

The mere act of putting on the Tefillin transforms the person. In the words of the Rambam, "The holiness of Tefillin is magnificent, for a person wearing Tefillin is awakened to humility, and elevated to be G-d fearing. He will not be persuaded toward callousness or to idol talk. His mind will not drift to negative thoughts, but rather his heart will be oriented towards words of truth and righteousness" *(Rambam. Hilchos Tefillin, 4:25)*.

Tefillin is our "confirmed document of freedom", it is like wearing the entire Torah. These five scrolls correspond to the five books of the Torah. The four individual scrolls in the Head Tefillin correspond to the first four books, and the one scroll in the Hand Tefillin corresponds to the final book of the Torah, which is a 'synopsis' of the other books. Just as a king of Israel would need to walk about with a Torah accompanying him, the same is true with us, as we are all 'children of kings'. By putting on Tefillin, we are carrying with us a Torah, the entire five books *(Sefas Emes, Bo)*.

Tefillin is the Malbush, 'garments', of the soul, rooted in Olam Ha'malbush, the 'world of Garments'. This is the inner, inner reality, even before the first Tzimtzum or 'cosmic contraction' *(Magid of Kaznitz)*.

"And it (the Tefillin) shall be for a sign to you on your arm, and a memorial between your eyes, so that the Torah of Hashem may be in your mouth..." *(Shemos, 13:9)*. This teaches us, says the S'mak, that even a non-righteous person who puts on Tefillin, through the very act of putting on and wearing the Tefillin, will be brought closer to the Torah, as it says, wrap the Tefillin "so that the Torah of Hashem may be in your mouth". The Tefillin bring a person to such a state *(S'mak)*.

The entire Torah is likened to Tefillin *(Kidushin, 35a)*. Tefillin encompasses both the value of the positive Mitzvos and the negative Mitzvos. A positive Mitzvah elevates creation through involvement, and refraining from negative actions elevates the denser levels of creation, that otherwise cannot be elevated, through abstaining. When we perform the positive Mitzvah of putting on Tefillin, and do so on the 'left/weaker' arm (which symbolizes 'negativity'), and place it on our head for all to see, we are elevating even the 'left' and 'outside' to G-d *(Likutei Sichos, 5)*.

"To one who is garbed in a Tallis and Tefillin, a heavenly voice rings out: "Give honor to the one who has the image of The King upon his head" *(Meam Loez, Ekev)*.

OTHER BOOKS BY
RAV DOVBER PINSON

REINCARNATION AND JUDAISM
The Journey of the Soul

A fascinating analysis of the concept of reincarnation as it appears in the works of the Kabbalistic masters, as well as how it is discussed by the great thinkers throughout history. Dipping into the fountain of ancient wisdom and modern understanding, the book addresses and answers such basic questions as: What is reincarnation? Why does it occur? and How does it affect us personally?

INNER RHYTHMS
The Kabbalah of Music

Exploring the inner dimension of sound and music, and particularly, how music permeates all aspects of life. The topics range from Deveikus/ Unity, Yichudim/ Unifications, to the more personal issues, such as Simcha/Happiness, and Marirus/ sadness.

MEDITATION AND JUDAISM
Exploring the Jewish Meditative Paths

A comprehensive work on Jewish meditation, encompassing the entire spectrum of Jewish thought—from the early Kabbalists to the modern Chassidic and Mussar masters, the sages of the Talmud to the modern philosophers.

The book is both a scholarly, in-depth study of meditative practices, and a practical, easy to follow guide for any person interested in meditating the Jewish way. In addition, the book broadens our view of meditation, demonstrating that in addition to the traditional methods of meditation ,meditation is prevalent within so many of the common Jewish practices.

TOWARD THE INFINITE
The Way of Kabbalistic Meditation

A book focusing exclusively on the Kabbalistic – Chassidic, Hisbonenus approach to meditation. Encompassing the entire meditative experience, it takes the reader on a comprehensive and engaging journey through meditation. The book explores the various states of consciousness that a person encounters in the course of the meditation, beginning at a level of extreme self-awareness and concluding with a total state of non-awareness.

JEWISH WISDOM OF THE AFTERLIFE
The Myths, the Mysteries & Meanings

What happens to us after we physically die? What is consciousness? And can it survive without a physical brain? What is a soul? Can we remember our past lives? Do near-death-experiences prove the immortality of the soul? Drawing from the fountain of ancient Jewish wisdom and modern understanding of what consciousness is, this book explores the possibilities of surviving death, the near-death-experience, and a possible glimpse of the peace and unconditional love that awaits, empowering the reader to live their day-to-day life with these great spiritual truths.

UPSHERIN
Exploring the Laws, Customs & Meanings
of a Boy's First Haircut

What is the meaning of Upsherin, the traditional celebration of a boy's first haircut at the age of three? This in-depth answer to that question explores as well the questions: Why is a boy's hair allowed to grow freely for his first three years? What is the kabbalistic import of hair in all its lengths and varieties? What is the mystical meaning of hair coverings? Rav DovBer Pinson answers these questions with his trademark deep learning and spiritual sensitivity. Includes a guide to conducting an Upsherin ceremony.

THIRTY – TWO GATES OF WISDOM
Awakening through Kabbalah

Kabbalah holds the secrets to a path of conscious awareness. In this compact book, Rav DovBer Pinson presents
32 key concepts of Kabbalah and shows their value in
opening the gates of perception.

THE PURIM READER
The Holiday of Purim Explored

With a Persian name, a costuming dress code and a
woman as the heroine, Purim is certainly unusual amongst
the Jewish holidays. Most people are very familiar with
the costumes, Megilah and revelry, but are mystified by
their significance. Rav DovBer Pinson offers a glimpse
into the unknown world of Purim, uncovering the mysteries and offering a deeper understanding of this unique
holiday.

EIGHT LIGHTS
8 Meditations for Chanukah

What is the meaning and message of Chanukah? What
is the spiritual significance of the Lights of the Menorah?

What are the Lights telling us? What is the deeper dimension of the Dreidel? Rav DovBer Pinson, with his trademark deep learning and spiritual sensitivity guides us through eight meditations relating to the Lights of the Menorah and the eight days of Chanukah, and a deeper exploration of the Dreidel.

Includes a detailed how-to guide for lighting the Chanukah Menorah

THE IYYUN HAGGADAH
An Introduction to the Haggadah

In this beautifully written introduction to Passover and the Haggadah, Rav DovBer Pinson, guides us through the major themes of Passover and the Seder night. Rav Pinson addresses the important questions, such as; What is the big deal of Chametz? What are we trying to achieve through conducting a Seder? What's with all that stuff on the Seder Plate? And most importantly, how is this all related to freedom? His answers will surprise even those who think they already know the answers to these questions.

THE MYSTERY OF KADDISH
Understanding the Mourner's Kaddish

The Mystery of Kaddish is an in-depth and Kabbalistic exploration into the Mourner's Kaddish Prayer. Throughout Jewish history, there have been many rites and rituals associated with loss and mourning, yet none have prevailed quite like the Mourner's Kaddish Prayer - which has become the definitive ritual of mourning. The book explores the source of this prayer and deconstructs the meaning to better understand the grieving process and how the Kaddish prayer supports and uplifts the bereaved through their own personal journey to healing.

RECLAIMING THE SELF
The Way of Teshuvah

Teshuvah is one of the great gifts of life. It speaks of a hope for a better today and empowers us to choose a brighter tomorrow. But what exactly is Teshuvah? And how does it work? How can we undo our past and how do we deal with guilt? And what is healthy regret without eroding our self-esteem? In this fascinating and empowering book, world-renowned teacher and thinker, Rav DovBer Pinson lays out a path for genuine transformation and a way to include all of our past in the powerful moment of the now.

PASSPORT TO KABBALAH
A Journey of Inner Transformation

Life is a journey full of ups and downs, inside-outs, and unexpected detours. There are times when we think we know exactly where we want to be headed, and other times when we are so lost we don't even know where we are. Rooted in the teachings of Kabbalah, this book provides readers with a passport of sorts to help them through any obstacles along their path of self-refinement, reflection, and self-transformation.

THE FOUR SPECIES
The Symbolism of the Lulav & Esrog

The Four Species, have inspired countless commentaries and traditions and intrigued scholars and mystics alike. In this little masterpiece of wisdom both profound and practical - Rav DovBer Pinson explores the deep symbolic roots and nature of the Four Species. The Na'anuim, or ritual of the Lulav movement, is meticulously detailed and Kavanos, or meditations, are offered for use with the practice. Includes an illustrated guide to the Lulav Movements.

A BOND FOR ETERNITY
Understanding the Bris Milah

What exactly is the Bris, the covenant, and what does it signify? Why on the eight day? Why the male? Why tamper with perfection? Rav DovBer Pinson, with his trademark deep learning reveals some of the deeper significance and hidden symbolism of the Bris.

THE GARDEN OF PARADOX:
The Essence of Non Dual Kabbalah

This book is a Primer on the Essential Philosophy of Kabbalah, presented as a series of 3 conversations, revealing the mysteries of Creator, Creation and Consciousness. With three representational students, embodying respectively, the philosopher, the activist and the mystic, Rav DovBer Pinson tackles the larger questions of life. Who is G-d? Who am I? Why do I exist? What is my purpose in this life? Written in clear and concise prose, Rav DovBer Pinson gently guides the reader towards making sense of life's paradoxes and living meaningfully.

ABOUT THE AUTHOR

Rav DovBer Pinson is a world-renowned Torah scholar, prolific author, and beloved spiritual teacher. He is widely recognized as one of the world's foremost authorities on authentic Kabbalah and Jewish wisdom.

Through his books, lectures and seminars he has touched and inspired the lives of thousands the world over.

He is the Rosh Yeshivah of the IYYUN Yeshiva and Dean of the IYYUN Center in Brownstone Brooklyn, NY.

www.ingramcontent.com/pod-product-compliance
Lightning Source LLC
Chambersburg PA
CBHW030506100426

42813CB00002B/366